Environmentally Sustainable Industrial Development in China

There is a growing concern among Chinese researchers and policymakers about China's industrial development being unsustainable and the irreversible depletion of natural resources and deterioration of the ecological environment. The relationship between industrial development, pollution and the environmental quality is an important issue that deserves careful study. Environmental considerations play a crucial role in shaping China's development strategies. Green development of China creates strong pressures for continuous transforming, upgrading and restructuring of the Chinese economy. This book explores how China's industrial development relates to pollution and environmental quality, and how considerations about such issues associated with the ecological system affect China's development strategies.

Yanqing Jiang is Professor of Economics at the School of Economics and Finance, Shanghai International Studies University, China. He received his PhD in economics from the Hanken School of Economics in Finland. His research works include over 50 journal articles and 10 research monographs published by well-known academic publishers.

Xu Yuan is a graduate student in economics at the School of Economics and Finance, Shanghai International Studies University, China. Her main research field is environmental economics. She has published several academic papers in various journals such as *Resources Guide*, *Resources Economization and Comprehensive Utilization*, and *Environmental Impact Assessment*.

Routledge Focus on Economics and Finance

The fields of economics are constantly expanding and evolving. This growth presents challenges for readers trying to keep up with the latest important insights. Routledge Focus on Economics and Finance presents short books on the latest big topics, linking in with the most cutting-edge economics research.

Individually, each title in the series provides coverage of a key academic topic, whilst collectively the series forms a comprehensive collection across the whole spectrum of economics.

The Malaysian Banking Industry
Policies and Practices after the Asian Financial Crisis
Rozaimah Zainudin, Chan Sok Gee and Aidil Rizal Shahrin

Automation, Capitalism and the End of the Middle Class
Jon-Arild Johannessen

Cryptocurrencies
A Primer on Digital Money
Mark Grabowski

Knowledge Infrastructure and Higher Education in India
Kaushalesh Lal and Shampa Paul

What Drives China's Economy
Economic, Socio-Political, Historical and Cultural Factors
Qing-Ping Ma

Environmentally Sustainable Industrial Development in China
Yanqing Jiang and Xu Yuan

For more information about this series, please visit www.routledge.com/Routledge-Focus-on-Economics-and-Finance/book-series/RFEF

Environmentally Sustainable Industrial Development in China

Yanqing Jiang and Xu Yuan

LONDON AND NEW YORK

First published 2020
by Routledge
2 Park Square, Milton Park, Abingdon, Oxon OX14 4RN

and by Routledge
52 Vanderbilt Avenue, New York, NY 10017

Routledge is an imprint of the Taylor & Francis Group, an informa business

© 2020 Yanqing Jiang and Xu Yuan

The right of Yanqing Jiang and Xu Yuan to be identified as authors of this work has been asserted by them in accordance with sections 77 and 78 of the Copyright, Designs and Patents Act 1988.

All rights reserved. No part of this book may be reprinted or reproduced or utilised in any form or by any electronic, mechanical, or other means, now known or hereafter invented, including photocopying and recording, or in any information storage or retrieval system, without permission in writing from the publishers.

Trademark notice: Product or corporate names may be trademarks or registered trademarks, and are used only for identification and explanation without intent to infringe.

British Library Cataloguing-in-Publication Data
A catalogue record for this book is available from the British Library

Library of Congress Cataloging-in-Publication Data
Names: Jiang, Yanqing, author. | Yuan, Xu, author.
Title: Environmentally sustainable industrial development in China / Yanqing Jiang and Xu Yuan.
Description: First Edition. | New York : Routledge, 2020. | Series: Routledge focus on economics and finance | Includes bibliographical references and index.
Identifiers: LCCN 2019054396 (print) | LCCN 2019054397 (ebook)
Subjects: LCSH: Industries—Environmental aspects—China. | Economic development—China. | Environmental policy—China.
Classification: LCC HC430.E5 J5386 2020 (print) | LCC HC430.E5 (ebook) | DDC 338.951/07—dc23
LC record available at https://lccn.loc.gov/2019054396
LC ebook record available at https://lccn.loc.gov/2019054397

ISBN: 978-0-367-19625-7 (hbk)
ISBN: 978-0-429-20338-1 (ebk)

Typeset in Times New Roman
by Apex CoVantage, LLC

Contents

List of figures vii
List of tables viii
Preface ix
Acknowledgements x

1   Introduction 1

2   Pollution and industrial development in China 4

   2.1   Pollution and the environment in China   5
   2.2   The impact of pollution on China's industrial development   13

3   Industrial development and environmental policy 16

   3.1   Basic characteristics of China's environmental policy   17
   3.2   Environmental policy evolution and industrial development   18
   3.3   Policy tools and industrial development in China   27
   3.4   Differential development and differentiated environmental policy   31

4   Environmental governance and sustainable development 36

   4.1   The effectiveness of China's environmental governance   36
   4.2   Policy defects and implications for sustainable development   39

vi Contents

    4.3 Policy issues and sustainable development 42
    4.4 Countermeasures for the implementation of environmental policy 48

5 **Industrial structure upgrading and environmental regulations in China**   57

    5.1 China's industrial structure and industrial development 57
    5.2 Environmental regulation and industrial development issues 64
    5.3 Policy recommendations 69

6 **China's role in environmental globalization**   89

    6.1 The main characteristics of environmental globalization 89
    6.2 Environmental policy innovation in countries around the world 91
    6.3 The dilemma faced by the governance system 97
    6.4 Suggestions on China's participation in global environmental governance 100

References   106
Index   108

Figures

2.1	Emissions of Major Pollutants from National Waste Gas	6
2.2	National Wastewater Discharge (100 million tons)	7
2.3	National General Industrial Solid Waste Production (10,000 tons)	8
2.4	The Proportion of National Nature Reserves (%)	10
2.5	Direct Economic Loss Caused by Geological Disasters	11
2.6	Typical Pollutant Emissions Levels by Province in 2017	12
2.7	Typical Pollutants in Different Regions of China in 2017	13
5.1	China's Three Major Industrial Output Values in 2008–2017	62

Tables

2.1	Emissions of Typical Pollutants in the Eastern, Central and Western Regions of China in 2017	12
3.1	Policies and Regulations in the Enlightenment Stage of Environmental Regulation in China (1972–1978)	19
3.2	Policies and Regulations at the Stage of Environmental System Construction (1979–1992)	20
3.3	Policies and Regulations in the Stage of Large-Scale Environmental Management (1993–2001)	22
3.4	Development of Environmental Regulations in the Phase of Integrated Environmental Management (2002–present)	25
5.1	China's Industrial Structure and Development (1981–2020)	59
5.2	GDP and the Three Major Industrial Output Values of China (100 million yuan)	61
5.3	Three Industrial Output Value Structures in the Eastern, Central and Western Regions of China (%)	63

Preface

This book discusses China's industrial development from an environmentally sustainable perspective within the general context of environmental globalization.

Over the past four decades, the spectacular economic growth and industrial development China has achieved has surprised the world. In just 40 years, China has leapt from one of the poorest countries to the second-largest economy in the world.

However, over this period of economic growth and industrial development, China has faced a growing concern that most developing countries also face, which is that the pattern of China's industrial development may not be environmentally sustainable because it may lead to irreversible depletion of natural resources and deterioration of the ecological environment. The relationship between industrial development, pollution and environmental quality is thus an important issue that deserves careful study. Environmental considerations play an important role in shaping China's development strategies. Environmentally sustainable development, or green development, of China creates strong pressures for continuous transforming, upgrading and restructuring of Chinese industries.

This book explores how China's industrial development is related to pollution and environmental quality, and how considerations about issues associated with the eco-environmental system may affect China's development strategies. The book presents to the reader facts, thoughts and discussions that shed light on those issues. This book will be of great interest to readers who are interested in environmentally sustainable industrial development in China.

Acknowledgements

The research contained in this book was carried out partly under the 2019–2020 funding of a key research project of Shanghai International Studies University. The authors thus thank the funding support provided by this project from Shanghai International Studies University.

1 Introduction

In 1978, the Third Plenary Session of the Eleventh Central Committee of the Communist Party of China (CPC) initiated the great historic process of China's reform and opening up. Over the past four decades, the tremendous achievements in reform and opening up have fundamentally changed the lives of the Chinese people. However, behind the rapid growth and development of the economy, there has been the trend of ecological environmental destruction and natural resource depletion. Obviously, China's economy and society have made remarkable achievements, but at huge environmental costs.

On September 7, 2013, President Xi Jinping said in a speech at Nazarbayev University in Kazakhstan: "We want not only gold and silver mountains, but also clean waters and green mountains because clean waters and green mountains are invaluable assets". It can be seen that the concept of "clean waters and green mountains are invaluable assets" is being implemented in China's economic construction and social development and is constantly pushing China's ecological civilization construction to a new level.

As the largest developing country in the world, along with its economic growth and social development over time, China's environmental pollution – that is, air pollution, water pollution and noxious waste pollution – has been enormous and cannot be underestimated. Ecological problems such as species extinction and soil erosion are also very serious. These and other environmental and ecological problems pose a serious threat to China's further development.

China's modern environmental policy has taken form since the 1972 United Nations Conference on the Human Environment. It has been more than 40 years since its inception. Along with the development of China's economy and social and public environmental awareness, the guiding ideology of China's environmental policy has undergone a development process from the basic national policy, the sustainable development strategy, the scientific concept of development, to the construction of ecological civilization. China's environmental policy has been changing accordingly with its guiding ideology. In the process of constant reflections and adjustments, China's environmental policy has constantly improved and gradually matured. In the past 40 years, the Chinese government has put more and more emphasis on environmental protection and environmentally sustainable industrial development. The government has continuously established, strengthened and updated laws and regulations on environmental protection and sustainable development. Through education and publicity, the Chinese government is committed to raising residents' awareness of environmental protection. Meanwhile, through incentives, administrative supervision and law enforcement, the government continuously improves its environmental protection and governance concepts of industrial development. Thus, the government plays an important role in China's environmental protection, sustainable industrial development and ecological civilization construction.

Owing to variations in environmental pollution and industrial development in different regions across China, the different characteristics of China's environmental problems have challenged China's environmental protection efforts in the new era. Consensus has been achieved that the traditional "one-size-fits-all" approach to environmental management cannot meet the needs of environmentally sustainable industrial development across China. In fact, China's environmental and industrial policies have continuously adapted to interregional differences. At present, China's environmental governance has improved a lot under the functioning of environmental policies. The total amount of pollutants discharged has continued to drop sharply, protections for the ecological environment have been strengthened and urban environmental quality has improved. However, China still faces serious environmental problems. One reason for this is that local governments and environmental management divisions are not always able to effectively implement environmental policies. Environmental policy implementation faces difficulties and challenges. Therefore, to strengthen environmental governance local governments must improve their implementation of environmental policies.

Industrial support and sustainable development are the meso-based foundation of a country's economic growth. The upgrading of industrial structure is an important issue in China's economic transformation and restructuring. Streamlining and upgrading the industrial structure, realizing the transformation of China's economic structure, taking the green development path of low pollution and low energy consumption and improving technology and total factor productivity are the starting points for China's economic development policy and strategic planning, as well as key factors for realizing the "win-win" situation of economic growth and environmental protection. On the one hand, China must strengthen its environmental laws and regulations to improve environmental quality. On the other hand, China should promote its economic transformation and upgrade its industrial structure. This is an important issue that must be solved soon in order to stimulate economic growth through the salutary interaction between China's environmental conditions and its industrial development.

Environmental globalization is an important feature of the era of globalization. Within the general framework of environmental globalization, China must be able to judge situations in a timely and accurate manner, striking a balance between tradeoffs in choosing policy tools and predicting the outcomes of policy innovation for the complex and diverse environmental and ecological problems the country faces. Moreover, China must have a firm and determined will to solve its environmental problems, to follow the correct direction of environmental innovations and to overcome the inertia in those innovations. China should give full play to its institutional advantages and fully realize that green, or environmentally sustainable, development is the only way to accelerate the construction of a resource-conserving and environment-friendly society and to increase prosperity for all.

Therefore, this book aims to introduce environmental policies with respect to the current situations of environmental pollution and industrial development in China. The book puts forward practical and feasible policy recommendations for improving China's environmental policies and for promoting the upgrading of its industrial structure. The book is organized as follows. Chapter 2 introduces the current situation of environmental pollution and ecological damages in China. Chapters 3 and 4 both focus on China's environmental policy. Chapter 3 gives a brief introduction to the basic development process and tools of China's environmental policy; Chapter 4 examines the defects and countermeasures of China's environmental governance. Based on this information, Chapter 5 discusses the linkages between China's environmental issues and its industrial development, focusing on how China should improve its environmental regulations and policies to promote the green development of its industrial structure. Finally, Chapter 6 analyzes the current situation and future trends of environmental globalization and discusses how China should shape its industrial development and participate in the process of environmental globalization.

2 Pollution and industrial development in China

Since the Industrial Revolution, mankind has made great achievements in economic development. However, with the development of economic globalization, industrial expansion and urbanization have caused great waste and destruction to the earth's resources and the environment; thus, economic growth has come at a great environmental cost. The constant plunder of resources and the pollution of the environment not only affect the longterm economic development of countries, but even threaten the survival of the entire human race. Although some scholars raised concerns about environmental protection issues as early as the 20th century, only in the last decade or so has the relationship between environmental development and economic development begun to receive the serious attention from the academic community, which has in turn led to extensive academic discussions.

The Chinese economy has experienced rapid growth in the approximately 40 years since the period of reform and opening up. Over this same period, the constraints of environmental resources on economic growth have become increasingly prominent. China's ecosystem has long been in a state of being overexploited. Many resources are gradually facing exhaustion owing to unrestricted exploitation in the process of economic growth, and the environment has rapidly deteriorated owing to lack of timely attention. Qu Geping, Chairman of the Environmental and Resource Protection Committee of the National People's Congress, has said more than once that the rapid growth of China's economy is largely based on the high consumption of resources and energy. This traditional development model has caused the deterioration of natural ecology (Huang, 2010).

At present, the implementation of sustainable development strategies has become the consensus of the international community. Economic and industrial development rely on the environment and natural resources. However, China's environmental situation is much more serious than previously thought. The scope and degree of ecological damage is expanding. As a result, in many places environmental pollution and ecological damage have restricted the sustainable, rapid and healthy development of the economy. It has become a serious problem with regard to economic and industrial development, further reform and opening up, as well as social stability. Therefore, effective measures to control environmental pollution must be implemented as soon as possible. In fact, the serious environmental pollution in China should be gradually solved in the process of industrial development.

2.1 Pollution and the environment in China

Environmental issues have always been the focus of the world. Global warming, energy shortages, air pollution, population expansion and species extinction have always had great influence on the living environment of mankind. In recent years, with China's rapid economic development and steady deepening of reform and opening up, the material living standards of the Chinese have improved significantly. However, behind the rapid economic development and improvement of the quality of material life, the environment in which we live is facing serious challenges. Although great progress has been made in environmental protection in China, the situation is still too serious. Environmental pollution and ecological destruction are harming industrial development and social stability in China.

2.1.1 Environmental pollution in China

As the largest developing country in the world, China's environmental pollution cannot be underestimated.

Air pollution is the most serious pollution in China. Current business operations, such as material plants, lime plants, foundries and so on, need to burn large amounts of coal and other fuels. When sulfur dioxide, a pollutant produced by coal combustion, is discharged into the atmosphere without effective treatment it has a negative impact on the atmosphere. Other harmful substances also impair the atmosphere's ability to self-purify. Reducing or eliminating the emission of pollutants caused by coal combustion is very costly. As a result, many factories choose to discharge toxic or harmful gases directly into the air, causing greater pollution in the atmosphere. In addition, with China's booming economy, people are increasing their use of a variety of multi-functional household appliances. These household appliances also generate large amounts of harmful gas emissions, which is another reason why the atmospheric environment has been severely polluted. At the same time, with the rapid development of China's automobile industry, more and more people are owning cars. Automobile exhaust has become one of the main causes of atmospheric environmental

6 Pollution and industrial development

pollution. Most obviously, this causes increasingly serious haze pollution every year (Xu, 2018). According to the data from cities such as Beijing, Shenyang, Xi'an, Shanghai and Guangzhou that participated in global atmospheric monitoring in 2010, the average annual concentration of total suspended particulate (TSP) was 200–500 micrograms/cubic meters, about three to six times more than the World Health Organization (WHO) health standard of 60–90 micrograms/cubic meters. Those five cities were listed among the 10 most polluted cities in the world. However, those five cities are only moderately polluted in China. Dust pollution in many cities is much more serious. For example, the daily average concentration of total suspended particulates in Jinan, Jilin, Taiyuan, Tongchuan and some other cities exceeds 1000 micrograms/cubic meters. About 70% of the 47 key cities in China failed to meet the second-level standards stipulated by the government. Of 338 cities that participated in an environmental survey, air quality in 137 cities exceeded the third-level national air quality standard, and are considered seriously polluted cities, accounting for 40% of the counted cities (for more details, see, e.g. Baidu Library and Figure 2.1).

Water pollution in China is a very serious problem. China also has a serious shortage of water resources. The total amount of freshwater resources in China is 280 billion cubic meters, which accounts for 6% of the world's

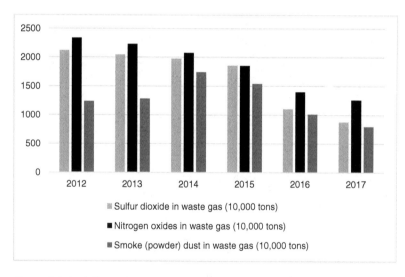

Figure 2.1 Emissions of Major Pollutants from National Waste Gas
Source: China Statistical Yearbook (various issues)

Pollution and industrial development 7

water resources. It ranks fourth in the world in total freshwater sources after Brazil, Russia and Canada. However, it has only 2200 cubic meters of freshwater per capita, which is only one fourth of the global average. China ranks 121st in the world with regard to freshwater per capita, and is one of the 13 countries with the poorest water resources per capita. Based on monitoring of seven river systems in China in 2001, only 29.5% of them met the Grade III water quality standard and the minimum requirements for entry to the waterworks, while the water quality of 44% of them was worse than Grade V. In addition, shallow groundwater pollution is relatively common in China. About 50% of shallow groundwater areas in China are polluted, and about half of those in urban areas are seriously polluted seriously. Owing to the wanton draining of industrial waste and residential sewage, more than 80% of surface water and groundwater is polluted. However, people are still wasting water resources despite the current situation of water pollution. The seven major rivers in China – the Hai, Liao, Huai, Yellow, Songhua, Yangtze and Pearl – are all polluted to varying degrees. The situation in the sea is problematic. Red tides occur every year. In the beautiful Bohai Bay, the water is turbid and oil pollution floats on the sea surface. According to the statistics, before July 2011 more than 400 of China's 660 cities, or two-thirds, were short of water. The annual water shortage in China's cities is about 6 billion cubic meters, and 110 cities are seriously short of water. For example, in the 1950s water wells in Beijing could be pumped out at about 5 meters below the surface. In contrast, the average depth of 40,000 wells in Beijing is 49 meters as a result of exhaustion of groundwater resources (for more details, see e.g. Baidu Encyclopedia and Figure 2.2).

Finally, noxious waste pollution is also a serious environmental problem in China. With the gradual improvement of people's living standards and the

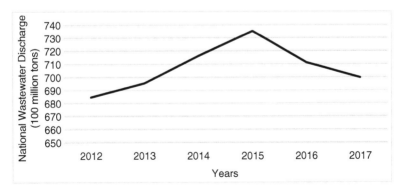

Figure 2.2 National Wastewater Discharge (100 million tons)
Source: China Statistical Yearbook (various issues)

8 *Pollution and industrial development*

increasing consumption of corresponding resources, noxious waste production in China has remained high for a long time, and is increasing rapidly at the rate of nearly 10% per year. About two-thirds of China's cities are trapped in the dilemma of garbage generation and removal. The annual production of "urban garbage" is nearly 150 million tons. Most of this urban garbage piles up in the open air and encroaches on a great quantity of land and introduces serious damage to the ecological environment. It not only affects the urban landscape, but also pollutes the atmosphere, water and soil and poses a threat to the health of urban residents. By 2013, the disposal rate of municipal solid waste above the county level in China had reached 89%, but there have been some significant shortcomings in recycling of construction and electronic waste. The annual output of industrial solid waste, e-waste, construction waste, waste metal, domestic waste and sludge from wastewater treatment plants is more than 4109 tons. However, the average utilization rate is less than 40%. A large mass of garbage has been accumulated, causing an enormous environmental burden. The garbage problem in urban areas has become a thorny problem in urban development. It causes not only a pollution nuisance, but also a huge waste of resources – the value of discarded renewable resources of 150 million tons of urban garbage is as high as 25 billion yuan every year. At present, a large number of garbage is dumped in landfills or incinerated without classification, and it is a huge waste of resources and a cause of secondary pollution. In addition, white pollution caused by plastic packaging and agricultural film has spread to almost all parts of China (see, for example, Ruan, 2011, and Figure 2.3).

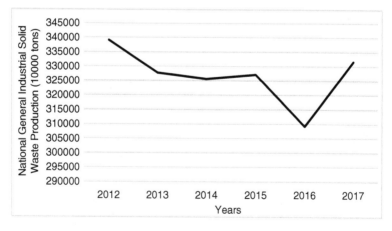

Figure 2.3 National General Industrial Solid Waste Production (10,000 tons)
Source: China Statistical Yearbook (various issues)

2.1.2 Industrial development and ecological damage in China

The situation of the ecological environment in China is becoming more serious. On the whole, the worsening trend of ecological deterioration has not been effectively curbed. The scope of damage to the ecological environment continues to increase. At the same time, the phenomena of "governance while destruction" and "destruction exceeding governance" still exist in many areas. The consequences of ecological destruction are serious. Species extinction and soil erosion are good examples for examining the current situation of ecological destruction in China.

Many species of animals and plants in China are under threat. Species extinction is an important manifestation of ecological destruction. China is one of the countries that has the broadest species diversity in the world. China is home to approximately 10% of species of higher plants and wildlife, of which about 200 are endemic. However, China is also a country experiencing serious losses of biodiversity. Environmental pollution and ecological destruction have led to the destruction of the environment on which animals and plants depend for their survival. The number of species has decreased dramatically, and many species are now extinct. According to statistics, approximately 4000–5000 species of higher plants are endangered, accounting for 15–20% of the total number of species in China, which is higher than the average global level of 10–15%. Of the 640 endangered species listed in the Convention on International Trade in Endangered Species of Wild Fauna and Flora, 156 are located in China, accounting for about a quarter of the total (Wang, Le & Zhang, 2006). Sadly, the phenomenon of hunting and killing wild animals indiscriminately in China is still very serious and difficult to prohibit. Figure 2.4 depicts the changing proportion of China's nature reserves over time.

Soil erosion is the most common geological hazard caused by damaged land in China. The total area of desertified land in China is 2,636,200 square kilometers. Sandstorms and desertified land have been continuously intensifying and expanding. From the late 1950s to the mid-1970s, area affected by desertification expanded by 1560 square kilometers on average per year, and the annual expansion from the mid-1970s to the late 1980s was 2100 square kilometers. By the end of the 1990s, it had grown to 3460 square kilometers per year. In the 70 years since the founding of the People's Republic of China, desert has expanded from 1.5 billion mu to 2.5 billion mu. There are 667,000 hectares of cultivated land, 2.35 million hectares of grassland and 6.39 million hectares of forest land that have become quicksand. The annual expansion rate of desertification is more than 4%. Owing to the sandstorms, people in many places have lost their homes and livelihoods,

10 *Pollution and industrial development*

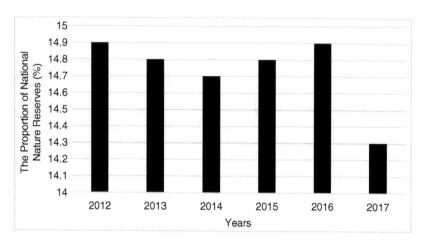

Figure 2.4 The Proportion of National Nature Reserves (%)
Source: China Statistical Yearbook (various issues)

becoming "ecological refugees". What is even more terrifying is that the Qinghai-Tibet Plateau has become a new source of sand. Desertified land on the Qinghai-Tibet Plateau has reached more than 500,000 square kilometers, accounting for 20% of the Qinghai-Tibet Plateau. Since the 1970s, there has been a net increase of 40,000 square kilometers, an increase of 8%. Qinghai Lake is shrinking day by day (Huang, 2010).Figure 2.5 shows the direct economic losses caused by geological disasters in China over time.

2.1.3 Differential development and pollution in different regions

Based on geographical location and economic development, China is divided into three major regions: eastern, central and western. According to the China Statistical Yearbook, the eastern region includes 11 provinces (cities): Beijing, Tianjin, Hebei, Liaoning, Shanghai, Jiangsu, Zhejiang, Fujian, Shandong, Guangdong and Hainan. The central region has 8 provincial-level administrative regions. They are Shanxi, Jilin, Heilongjiang, Anhui, Jiangxi, Henan, Hubei and Hunan. The western region has 12 provincial administrative regions, namely Sichuan, Chongqing, Guizhou, Yunnan, Tibet, Shaanxi, Gansu, Qinghai, Ningxia, Xinjiang, Guangxi and Inner Mongolia. China has a vast territory and a large population. The three regions differ significantly in natural conditions, level of economic development, level of opening up and social conditions. Regional development

Pollution and industrial development 11

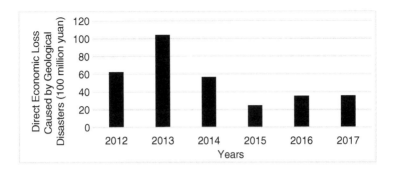

Figure 2.5 Direct Economic Loss Caused by Geological Disasters
Source: China Statistical Yearbook (various issues)

imbalances are widespread. Since the late 1990s China has successively introduced regional development strategies such as the Great Western Development Strategy, the Strategy of Promoting the Rise of Central China and the Northeast Rejuvenation Strategy, but the development gap between regions is still very large.

Table 2.1 provides typical pollutant emissions levels in the eastern, central and western regions of China in 2017, and Figure 2.6 depicts the percentage of typical pollutants in the eastern, central and western regions of China in 2017. Wastewater is an indicator of pollution that reflects water quality. Sulfur dioxide and nitrogen oxides are indicators of air quality. Solid waste pollution is related to water, air and soil pollution. It can be clearly seen from the table that with regard to these four types of pollutants there are differences between the eastern, central and western regions. In general, pollution is more serious in the eastern region than in the central and western regions. Except for sulfur dioxide emissions, which are slightly lower than those in the western region, the emissions of other pollutants are greater than those in the central and western regions. Compared with the western region, the central region has higher nitrogen oxide emissions and waste water, but less sulfur dioxide emissions and solid waste pollution. Given that the data is limited to 2017 and only four representative pollutants, the ranking of environmental pollution in the eastern, central and western regions cannot be determined, particularly given the fact that environmental pollution in various regions is constantly changing. The national environmental situation is critical, and environmental quality is still facing severe challenges. The Chinese government has begun to pay attention to the environmental impact of economic development.

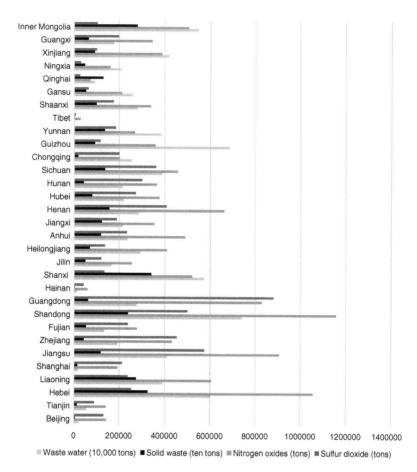

Figure 2.6 Typical Pollutant Emissions Levels by Province in 2017
Source: China Statistical Yearbook

Table 2.1 Emissions of Typical Pollutants in the Eastern, Central and Western Regions of China in 2017

Contaminant	Eastern region	Central region	Western region
Sulfur dioxide (tons)	2851634	2204853	3697865
Nitrogen oxides (tons)	5806664	3435734	3346192
Waste water (10,000 tons)	3620980	1800206	1575425
Solid waste (10,000 tons)	116593	98869	116126

Source: China Statistical Yearbook

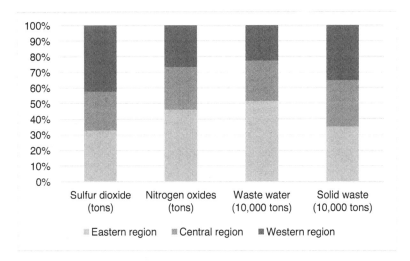

Figure 2.7 Typical Pollutants in Different Regions of China in 2017
Source: China Statistical Yearbook

2.2 The impact of pollution on China's industrial development

Environmental pollution has seriously hindered China's industrial development. In the 1990s, various organizations did relevant research work. The results showed that environmental losses (property losses and health losses) account for 3% to 4% of China's GDP. In addition, according to the estimates from the World Bank, the National Environmental Protection Agency and the Chinese Academy of Sciences, annual losses caused by environmental pollution in China account for about 10% of GDP. The "factory" economic model of the coastal cities in eastern China has undoubtedly been successful from an economic standpoint, making the coastal cities the richest places in China. However, this economic model has had a huge impact on local environmental pollution (Zhang, 2014). The constraints of the three major types of environmental pollutions on China's industrial development are as follows.

First, the impact of air pollution on the economy is prominent. Researchers in the field of environmental economic research estimate that economic losses due to the adverse effects of air pollution on human health account for about half of the economic losses due to environmental pollution. In 1995, the economic cost of adverse health effects due to air pollution in China reached 17.10 billion yuan, and over the past three years losses have grown to more than 600 billion yuan. Taking dioxin produced by waste incineration as an example, researchers at the Shanghai Academy of Public Measurement conducted research in 2008 on the vegetable planting base around an incineration plant and found that the dioxin content in the soil was higher than the reference value of dioxin content for agricultural soils formulated by Germany, the Netherlands, Sweden and other countries. Obviously, this has had a great impact on the development of local agriculture. In 2010, experts from Sichuan University and Shenzhen Center for Disease Control and Prevention also investigated the dioxin content of poultry products for sale in Shenzhen and found that some exceeded the values set by EU, which has restricted the sales of agricultural and sideline products in China.

Second, the impact of water pollution on the economy is even more difficult to ignore (Zhang, 2014). China's water resources are relatively scarce, with per capita freshwater resources being roughly a quarter of the global per capita value. With the development of industry and agriculture and the improvement of people's living standards, water shortages are becoming a serious problem, and water pollution has only intensified it. Water shortages will directly restrict the development of industry and agriculture. Consider the pollution of the Songhua River in 2005 as an example. An accidental explosion at PetroChina Jilin Petrochemical Company caused a major water pollution incident in the Songhua River. Local aquatic ecology, aquatic products, agricultural products, livestock and poultry products, water supply, landscape (tourist attractions) and residents were directly affected by water pollution. The resulting economic losses included loss of economic activity, expenditures on maintaining health, expenditures on restoration of water quality and economic losses due to disruptions in production, which is undoubtedly a considerable expenditure (Zhang, 2014).

Finally, the impact of solid waste pollution on the economy is enormous. Solid waste can undergo chemical, physical and biological transformation under certain conditions that will impact on the surrounding environment. If the treatment method is improper, harmful substances will endanger the environment and human health through contaminated water, air, soil and the food chain. Generally, the chemical components in industrial, mining and other wastes cause environmental pollution. In addition, human and animal manure and organic waste are breeding grounds for various pathogenic microorganisms, forming pathogen-type pollution.

There are generally four ways in which solid wastes pollute the environment. The first is contamination of soil. The storage of solid waste not only occupies a large amount of land, but also invites flies and dust. Toxic substances then spread everywhere due to weathering, and the toxic substances contained in the exudates will change the soil quality and soil structure, contaminating the soil. What's more, some pathogens are transmitted to people through plants, which threatens people's health. The second way that solid waste affects the environment is water pollution. Under the action of rainwater, solid waste can easily flow into rivers and lakes or penetrate into groundwater through soil, which causes serious pollution and damage. What is even worse is that solid waste is dumped directly into rivers, lakes and oceans, resulting in more serious pollution and poisoning large numbers of aquatic organisms. The third way solid waste affects the environment is pollution of the atmosphere. During the stacking process, certain organic substances are decomposed under the action of temperature and moisture and produce harmful gases. Some spoiled garbage wastes emit odor and cause pollution to the atmosphere. Some corrupt garbage wastes emit odor and cause pollution to the atmosphere. Finally, solid waste affects environmental sanitation. At present, some hospital waste is mixed with common garbage resulting in the potential spread of hepatitis, enteritis, dysentery and various helminthiasis (parasitic disease) and becoming a serious source of environmental pollution. In addition, most of the garbage in China is ash and dirty soil, which not only has low fertilizer efficiency but also makes the soil compact and reduces the yield of vegetable crops (Ruan, 2011).

The problem of environmental pollution has always been a major problem that has plagued the rapid development of China's economy. On the one hand, the rapid development of the economy, such as the construction of factories, will inevitably affect the environment. If there are no perfect measures to purify sewage, these factories will cause great damage to the environment. On the other hand, if the importance of environmental protection is overemphasized, it will inevitably hinder the speed of China's industrial development. Therefore, how to achieve rapid industrial development while protecting the environment and truly deal with both in a balanced manner is a problem that has to be considered carefully. At present, China is implementing the Great Western Development Strategy. As a result, China's economic center will gradually move westward, and large-scale factories with large pollution emissions will also be built in the west. It is necessary to develop the western economy and narrow the gap between the east and the west. But how to solve the environment problem and avoid the tragedy caused by the neglect of environmental protection due to economic development is also something that must be taken into account.

3 Industrial development and environmental policy

As the name of the chapter implies, environmental policy refers to the criteria for rational development and utilization of natural resources to protect and improve the environment in order to achieve harmonious development between man and nature. Through this definition, we can clearly understand the purpose behind environmental policies – to improve the relationship between people and nature, and to promote the coordinated development of human society and nature.

The 18th National Congress of the Communist Party of China incorporated the construction of ecological civilization into the overall layout of "five in one" of Socialism with Chinese Characteristics. It promoted the rapid development of China's environmental policy and made China's environmental policy objectives clearer, the system sounder, and the content more detailed (He, 2017). The report of the 19th National Congress of the Communist Party of China also pointed out that "it is necessary to create more material wealth and spiritual wealth to meet the people's growing needs for a better life, and to provide more high-quality ecological products to meet the people's growing needs for a beautiful ecological environment"(Xi, 2017). We know that disharmony between industrial development and environmental protection is currently the main contradiction that the country faces with regard to green governance. The government cannot shirk its responsibility for the country's industrial transformation and sustainable development. In order to formulate and successfully implement environmental policies, the central government should describe the development vision, build an institutional system and improve its ability in comprehensive green governance. However, local governments must also design proper policies and strengthen policy implementation. Local governments should adopt different policy tools for different types of environmental problems, by industry and by region, so as to avoid the negative impact of inappropriate "one-size-fits-all" environmental governance policies on local industry and economic development (Zhou, Zhang, Zhao, Chen & Xue, 2018).

3.1 Basic characteristics of China's environmental policy

It is generally believed that China's environmental policy, as guided by the Marxist ideology, is in general terms a series of actions and plans, rules, and measures and countermeasures implemented to improve and protect the ecological environment and prevent pollution based on current social and economic development and the actual situation of environmental protection. Environmental policy is not only an important basis for environmental protection work, but also an important means to coordinate the relationship between economic development and resources and the environment, which reflects the awareness of policy makers on the relationship between the environment and economic and social development. China's modern environmental policy started more than 40 years ago with the 1972 United Nations Conference on the Human Environment. With the development of China's economy, social progress and increased environmental awareness by the public, the guiding ideology of environmental policy has undergone a development process from a basic national policy, to a sustainable development strategy, to a scientific outlook on development and finally to ecological civilization. China's environmental policy has changed over time to reflect the guiding ideology. In the process of constant reflection and adjustment of the environmental policy, China's environmental policy has constantly improved and gradually matured.

The scope of China's environmental policy is very broad and includes laws and regulations on environmental and resource protection, policy documents on environmental and resource protection formulated by the Communist Party of China, documents on environmental resource protection jointly issued by state organs and the Communist Party of China, relevant environmental regulations formulated by Chinese state organs, and international laws and policy documents or the speeches, reports and directives made by the Party and state leaders at major conferences on environmental and resource protection. The environmental policy we usually mention refers to the narrow environmental policy which is the normative documents such as laws and regulations, departmental regulations and local regulations on environmental and resource protection.

From a hierarchical perspective, environmental policies can be divided into three levels: macro, meso and micro. The macro-environmental policy is the general guideline that guides environmental work steadily for a period of time. The meso-environmental policy is formulated around macroeconomic policies in order to guide some basic policies in one aspect of environmental protection. Micro-environmental policies are specific policy

18 *Industrial development and policy*

measures designed to address specific environmental issues. According to the field classification, environmental policies include environmental economic policies, environmental technology policies, environmental and social policies, environmental administrative policies and international environmental policies. Based on their implementation methods, environmental policies can be divided into command-control environmental policies, economic incentive environmental policies and public participation environmental policies (He, 2017).

3.2 Environmental policy evolution and industrial development

Two landmark events officially kicked off China's environmental regulation process: one was China's participation in the United Nations Conference on the Human Environment in Stockholm, Sweden, in 1972, while the other was the first national environmental protection conference held in China in 1973. By 2019, China's environmental regulations had gone through 47 years of development. Over this period, the Chinese government has viewed environmental protection as an increasingly important task and has been continuously establishing and improving relevant laws and regulations on environmental protection. Through education and publicity, the government is committed to raising residents' awareness of environmental protection. Through incentives, administrative supervision and law enforcement, the government continuously improves the environmental protection and governance concepts of enterprise development. In short, the Chinese government has gradually improved the environmental regulation system in the practice of environmental regulation construction, and has played an important role in China's environmental protection and ecological civilization construction. According to the research viewpoint in the China Sustainable Development Report (2013), the history of development of environmental regulation in China can be divided into four stages: the enlightenment stage of environmental regulation (1972–1978), the stage of environmental system construction (1979–1992), the stage of large-scale environmental management (1993–2001) and the stage of integrated environmental management (2002–present).

The first phase is the enlightenment stage of environmental regulation (1972–1978). In June 1972, China sent a delegation to participate in the first meeting of the United Nations Conference on the Human Environment in Stockholm, Sweden. With this meeting, the Chinese government began to realize that China faced serious ecological and environmental problems and needed to pay attention to environmental protection. In 1973, China held the first National Environmental Protection Conference and passed the Provisions on the Protection and Improvement of the Environment, the first policy document on environmental protection in China. The conference also formulated crucial guidelines for environmental protection in China, namely, "comprehensive planning, rational distribution, comprehensive utilization, turning harm into benefit, relying on the masses, everyone acting together, protecting the environment and benefiting the people". This meeting marked the official start of environmental regulation in China. In October 1974, the Environment Protection Leading Group of the State Council was established. Subsequently, every province, autonomous region and municipality established environmental protection management agencies, monitoring institutions and scientific research institutions to carry out environmental protection and governance work. Up to the reform and opening up in 1978, China successively promulgated relevant policies, laws and regulations, laying an important foundation for China's environmental regulation work. Table 3.1 provides a summary of the enlightenment stage of environmental regulation (for a more detailed discussion, see Shi, 2017).

Table 3.1 Policies and Regulations in the Enlightenment Stage of Environmental Regulation in China (1972–1978)

Date	Policy (Regulations and Documents)	Role and Importance
August 1973	Provisions on the Protection and Improvement of the Environment	China's first environmental protection document, marking the official start of environmental regulation in China.
November 1973	Trial Standards for the Emission of "Three Wastes" from Industry	China's first environmental standard provided a policy basis for the implementation of the "three wastes" governance.
April 1977	Several Provisions on the Comprehensive Utilization of Industrial "Three Wastes"	China entered a new stage of development in the work of harnessing industrial "three wastes" and comprehensive utilization.
February 1978	The Constitution of the People's Republic of China provides provisions on the ecological environment such as the environment, natural resource protection and pollution prevention	The first time the Chinese government had clearly defined environmental protection in the Constitution, laying a legal foundation for China's environmental protection legal system construction and environmental regulation.

20 *Industrial development and policy*

The second phase is environmental system construction (1979–1992). With China's reform and opening up, the rapid development of China's township and village enterprises between 1984 and 1988 had a major impact on China's ecological environment. According to the statistics of the National Environmental Protection Agency, China entered the high-emission stage of air pollutants in 1986. China's sulfur dioxide emissions in 2002 were 12.08 million tons, which exceeded the environmental capacity of 12 million tons of sulfur dioxide measured by the Chinese Academy of Environmental Planning. During the Sixth Five-Year Plan period (1981–1985), China's environmental protection investment accounted for about 0.52% of GDP. Investment in environmental protection was low and the work involved was difficult. Although the basic national policy of environmental protection had been established in this period and environmental regulation had entered the stage of legalization, the work of environmental protection could hardly meet the actual needs. However, the good thing was that during this stage China further promulgated policies and regulations on environmental protection and the framework for an environmental regulation system was constructed and developed. For example, during this period the environmental impact assessment system and the environmental pollution control system were established. The main environmental protection work used command-control environmental regulation tools. Table 3.2 summarizes the stage of environmental system construction (for a more detailed discussion, see Shi, 2017).

The third stage is large-scale environmental management (1993–2001). In 1992, China established the goal of reforming the market economic

Table 3.2 Policies and Regulations at the Stage of Environmental System Construction (1979–1992)

Date	Policy (Regulations and Documents)	Role and Importance
September 1979	Environmental Protection Laws of the People's Republic of China (Trial) Implemented environmental impact assessment and sewage charge system.	Policy clearly stated that environmental protection was an important part of socialist modernization construction and stipulates the environmental impact assessment system for the first time. This is China's first basic law on environmental protection, marking the official entry into the legalization stage of China's environmental regulation.

Industrial development and policy 21

Date	Policy (Regulations and Documents)	Role and Importance
April 1989	Environmental Protection Laws of the People's Republic of China (Trial) Put forward five new systems: objective responsibility for environmental protection, quantitative assessment of the comprehensive improvement of the urban environment, application for registration and emission permits, centralized control, undertaking of treatment within a prescribed time period	China's environmental regulations became more institutionalized and scientific.
1992	Ten Strategies for Environment and Development	For the first time, China clearly proposed changing the traditional development model and taking the road of sustainable development.
	China's Agenda 21 China Environmental Protection Action Plan	Put forward the strategy of sustainable development.

system, which accelerated the pace of reform and opening up in China. After 1992, China set off on a new round of economic growth, but it was clearly accompanied by high pollution and high emissions. During this period, the main types of air pollutants in China were soot, mainly total suspended particulate matter and sulfur dioxide. Acid rain pollution often occurred in cities in southern China. In 1995, China's sulfur dioxide emissions were 18.91 million tons, an increase of 50% compared with the 12.08 million tons of sulfur dioxide emissions in 1986. However, during the Asian financial crisis of 1997–2000, China's emissions of environmental pollutants decreased. One reason for this may be that economic growth in China was affected by the Asian financial crisis, resulting in reduced emissions. It may also reflect the stricter supervision and enforcement of regulatory objectives of the environmental protection department compared with the previous period that resulted in the shutting down of a number of high-pollution enterprises. Thus, industrial restructuring had a direct impact on environmental protection during this period. After 1997 the central government held three working conferences on population, resources and environmental issues, emphasizing the establishment and improvement of comprehensive environmental and development decision-making, unified supervision and division of responsibilities, environmental investment and

22 *Industrial development and policy*

public participation. In 2000, China's investment in environmental governance accounted for 1% of GDP for the first time, but it was still a drop in the bucket compared with the actual demand for environmental regulation work. It important to note that beginning with the Asian financial crisis the Chinese government started to use fiscal policy to promote the economy by issuing large-scale treasury bonds in order to ensure that the economic growth rate was above 8%. A large part of the funds was used for environmental infrastructure construction, which is the first time that the Chinese government invested in environmental infrastructure construction on a large scale. From 1998 to 2002, the Chinese government issued a total of 660 billion yuan of government bonds, of which 65 billion yuan was used to support urban environmental infrastructure construction. As a result, 603 sewage treatment projects, 22 new water reuse projects and 164 garbage disposal projects were implemented. In this stage, China gradually formed a Chinese model of environmental regulation and began to implement large-scale environmental protection and pollution control measures (Shi, 2017). Although great achievements were made in this stage, the ecological environment had been seriously damaged. The pollution problem was not resolved. The characteristics of "high pollution, high energy consumption and deteriorating ecological environment" continued to be a feature of China's economic and social development. Table 3.3 gives a summary of this phase (for a more detailed discussion, see Shi, 2017).

The fourth phase is integrated environmental management (2002–present). China formally joined the World Trade Organization (WTO) in 2002.

Table 3.3 Policies and Regulations in the Stage of Large-Scale Environmental Management (1993–2001)

Date	Policy (Regulations and Documents)	Role and Importance
October 1993	The Second Working Conference on Industrial Pollution Control put forward that cleaner production and "three transformations" must be implemented in industrial pollution prevention and control.	This marks a change in the guidelines for the prevention and control of industrial pollution in China.
July 1994	Administrative Measures for Certification of Environmental Products (Trial)	Start of China's environmental labeling work. Information disclosure and participation mechanisms were applied in China's environmental regulation policies.

Industrial development and policy 23

Date	Policy (Regulations and Documents)	Role and Importance
July 1996	Decision of the State Council on Several Issues Concerning Environmental Protection, Total Emission Amount and Control Plan, China's over Century Green Project	The objectives, tasks and measures of trans-century environmental protection work were clarified.
1999	State Environmental Protection Administration (SEPA) carried out pilot work on sulfur dioxide emission trading in Nantong, Jiangsu Province, and Benxi, Liaoning Province.	China's market-based environmental regulations began to explore and develop in a diversified way.
	Implementation Measures for Establishing ISO14000 National Demonstration Zones	The beginning of environmental certification in China. The information disclosure and participation mechanism, an environmental regulation policy tool, was further developed.
September 2001	The sulfur dioxide emissions trading system funded by the Asian Development Bank was piloted in Taiyuan, Shanxi	Promoted the implementation of the emissions trading system, a market-based environmental regulation tool in China.

Beginning in 1992, China's openness to trade expanded and it gradually entered the world economic arena. Upon joining the WTO, China's economy continued to grow at a high speed, and the volume of trade and foreign direct investment in China increased significantly. However, the ecological and environmental problems in China have become increasingly complex and the ecological environment has begun to deteriorate. As China expanded its opening up to the outside world, some polluting industries and products were gradually transferred from other countries or regions to China through the transmission path of foreign trade and foreign direct investment. Given that the eastern part of China is relatively open compared to the central and western regions and it was the main area for China's opening up of early trade and foreign direct investment, the eastern region has been a "pollution shelter" for a long time. In addition, since the second half of 2002 China has witnessed a boom in heavy chemical industry. High-pollution and high-energy–consuming industries such as steel, cement, chemicals, chemical industry, coal and electricity have sprung up. Large-scale exploitation of resources and energy consumption resulted in a jump in industrial sulfur dioxide emissions from 16.13 million tons in 2000 to 22.276 million tons in 2006, and an increase in industrial chemical oxygen demand emissions from 7.05 million tons in 2000 to 14.28 million tons in 2006. Emissions remain high, and China's resource and environmental problems have become increasingly severe. Environmental problems in China were particularly serious during the 10th Five-Year Plan period (2001–2005), and environmental protection targets were not achieved. Since 2002, China's environmental problems have shifted from localized and single-type pollution to more global and complex pollution from low-deteriorating countries to high-deteriorating countries (Shi, 2017). Unfortunately, China followed the old road of "treatment after pollution first" used in Western developed countries.

From 2002 to 2018, China's investment in environmental governance accounted for about 1–1.7% of GDP. Most of the investment was used for urban environmental infrastructure construction, which reflected the improvement of the government's command-control environmental regulation. However, according to the experience of the United States and Japan in environmental governance, the proportion of investment in environmental governance should be at least 2–3% of GDP. This shows that China's current environmental governance investment has not yet reached the lower limit of the actual investment required for environmental pollution control in China.

China began to carry out pilot work for a discharge permit system in 2004. The sewage discharge permit effectively linked the relationship between the environmental protection administrative department and the pollutant discharge enterprise, reflecting the further development of China's command-control environmental regulation. On the other hand, as for environmental protection taxes and fees, China increased the collection of sewage charges and expanded the scope of payment of sewage charges in 2003. The reform of ad valorem taxation of crude oil and natural gas resources was implemented in Xinjiang in 2010. The reform of ad valorem taxation of coal resources tax was implemented nationwide in December 2014. China comprehensively implemented the reform of ad valorem taxation of resources tax and clarified the fee fund in July 2016, which further improved the green tax system. China passed the Environmental Protection Tax Law on December 25, 2016 and set up a transition period of more than a year, such that it was officially implemented on January 1, 2018. In short, China's resource and environmental taxation system has been continuously reformed and improved over the years and China's resource and environmental issues are closely linked with the market, reflecting the improvement and development of China's market-based environmental regulation. Table 3.4 gives a summary of this phase (for a more detailed discussion, see Shi, 2017).

According to the development process of China's environmental policy mentioned above, Professor Zhang Kunmin, the general consultant of the

Table 3.4 Development of Environmental Regulations in the Phase of Integrated Environmental Management (2002–present)

Date	Policy (Regulations and Documents)	Role and Importance
October 2002	The Environmental Impact Assessment Law states that the opinions of the units, experts and the public on the environmental impact assessment report should be sought to avoid adverse impacts on the environment.	Established public participation in environmental regulation.
July 2003	The Administrative Measures on the Collection and Use of Sewage Charges was officially implemented.	Further improved the sewage charge system and promoted the development of market-based environmental regulation.
2004	Notice on the Launch of Pilot Projects in Pollution Discharge Permits	Implemented the sewage permit system and used it as an important means of environmental pollution control, which further strengthened command-control environmental regulation.
	Interim Measures for Hearing the Administrative License in Respect of Environmental Protection	Marked the formal implementation of the environmental hearing system with public participation.
February 2006	Interim Measures for Public Participation in Environmental Impact Assessment	Public participation in environmental regulation was further improved and developed.
2010	Provisions on Several Issues of Xinjiang Crude Oil and Natural Gas Resources Tax Reform	Improved China's green taxation system, closely linked resource taxes with prices and effectively linked resource and environmental issues with the market. Further improved and developed market-based environmental regulation.
December 2014	Notice on the Reform of Coal Resource Tax	
July 2016	Notice on Expanding Reform of Resource Tax Resource tax implementation of comprehensive ad valorem taxation	
December 2016	12th National People's Congress voted to pass the Environmental Protection Tax Law	This was the first single-line tax law introduced by China after the 18th National Congress of the Communist Party of China. It established a cooperation mechanism between the green taxation system and environmental protection work and further developed China's market-oriented environmental regulations.
January 2018	Environmental Protection Tax Law is officially implemented	

26 *Industrial development and policy*

National Environmental Protection Bureau, noted five changes that China's environmental policy has undergone over the years:

1   The status of China's environmental policy has changed from a basic national policy to a sustainable development strategy. At the end of 1983, the State Council declared that environmental protection is a basic national policy of China. In this way, environmental and population issues are placed in an equally important and urgent position. In 1992, Ten Strategies for China's Environment and Development announced the implementation of the sustainable development strategy. After the publication of China's Agenda 21 in 1994, different departments and localities have formulated their own and local Agenda 21 and promoted its implementation from different aspects such as planning, regulations, policies, communication and public participation. In 1996, the Ninth Five-Year Plan put sustainable development and developing the country through science and education as two basic strategies. Most departments in most provinces and cities in China have achieved development planning with the goal of sustainable development and guided the work of the department or the region through the concept of unity of environment and development.
2   The emphasis of China's environmental policy has shifted from focusing on pollution control to paying equal attention to pollution control and ecological protection. In the early 1970s, environmental protection in China started from the treatment of industrial wastewater, waste gas and solid waste. In the 1980s and early 1990s the focus was still on pollution control. In 1998, after the extraordinary floods in the Yangtze River, the state implemented a series of policy measures to protect the natural ecology, such as comprehensively stopping the logging of natural forests in the upper and middle reaches of the Yangtze River and the Yellow River, ranking ecological restoration and construction as the primary measures for the great western development strategy, the policy of "returning farmland to forests and grasslands, sealing mountains and greening, selling by grain, and individual contracting" was formulated and so on. This marks a historic turn in China's environmental policy – from the early emphasis on pollution control to the emphasis on both pollution control and ecological protection after 1998.
3   The approach of China's environmental policy has changed from "end-of-pipe treatment" to "containment from the source". In the early 1990s, industrial pollution control in China began to change from "end-of-pipe treatment" to whole process control, from simple concentration control to combination of concentration and total amount control, and from decentralized treatment to combination of decentralized and

centralized treatment. China has restricted the development of industries with high resource consumption, heavy pollution and backward technology and used the World Bank loan to start the pilot project of cleaner production.
4 The scope of China's environmental policy ranges from point source control to river basin and regional environmental management. Before 1996, China implemented the policy of "who pollutes and who governs", focusing on point source control and concentration control. China implemented the China's over Century Green Project from 1996 to 2005, which focused on the "Three Rivers", "Three Lakes", "Two Areas" (SO_2 Pollution Control Zone and Acid Rain Control Zone), "One City" (Beijing) , "One Sea" (Bohai Sea), and the Three Gorges Reservoir Area and its upstream and as well as South-to-North Water Diversion areas. In 2006, the Yellow River and Songhua River were also included. Obviously, the scope of China's environmental policy has changed from point source to watershed and regional environmental governance.
5 The main governance methods of China's environmental policy have changed from administrative orders to legal and economic means. Since the 1990s, China's environmental legal system has been continuously strengthened. The provincial, district, municipal people's congresses and governments have promulgated more than 1600 local environmental laws and regulations and basically forming an environmental law system. But it still needs further improvement. In order to strengthen the incentive effect of economic means, the relevant departments of the State Council formulate and improve economic policies and measures conducive to environmental protection in terms of capital construction, comprehensive utilization, fiscal taxation, financial credit and introduction of foreign investment.

(Zhang, Wen & Peng, 2007)

3.3 Policy tools and industrial development in China

3.3.1 Types of environmental policy tools in China

Public policy instruments, also known as governmental tools or governance tools, are specific ways and means that people use to solve a social problem or achieve certain policy goals. Thus, environmental policy tools are the means people use to solve environmental problems or reach a certain environmental policy goal. The application of environmental policy tools is indispensable for achieving certain environmental policy objectives and environmental governance.

28 Industrial development and policy

In China, environmental policy instruments are generally divided into command-control environmental policy tools, economic incentive environmental policy tools and public participation environmental policy tools. Command-control tools, also known as direct control tools, are designed to limit the emissions of specific pollutants by managing production processes or product use. It is an institutional measure that directly limits the environmental damage of certain polluters at specific times and in certain regions. The main feature of institutional measures is the regulation of pollution emissions. Economic incentive environmental policy tools are also known as market-based environmental policy tools. The motivation for adopting economic incentive tools is that if the parties think that adopting more environmentally friendly behaviors means more economic benefits, their attitudes and behaviors will turn "automatically" in a direction that is more conducive to environmental protection. Public participatory environmental policy tools use methods such as education, information dissemination, training, social pressure, negotiation and other forms of "moral education" to promote environmental protection. The specific analysis of various types of environmental policy tools in China is as follows.

China's command-control environmental policy tools include the following:

1 Environmental planning system: Based on the implementation of the Environmental Protection Law (1989) environmental authorities above the county level have to formulate environmental protection plans and incorporate them into the national economic and social development plans of the region. Environmental planning focuses on the prevention of environmental problems, which reflects the principle of environmental protection prevention.
2 Three simultaneous systems: When installing environmental protection facilities at all newly built, rebuilt and expanded capital construction projects (including small-scale construction projects, technological transformation projects, natural development projects, regional development projects and projects that may cause damage to the environment), it must be designed, constructed and put into operation at the same time as the main project.
3 Environmental impact assessment system: Environmental impact assessment is to measure and evaluate the possible environmental impacts of the proposed construction project, regional development plan and international policy implementation.
4 Discharge permit system: This is a system aimed at improving environmental quality. It is based on total pollutant control and has specific regulations on the types, quantities, properties, directions and modes

Industrial development and policy 29

of pollutant discharge. It is an administrative management system with legal meaning. At present, China mainly implements the water pollutant discharge permit system.

5 Centralized pollution control system: This is a policy-oriented and managerial technical means for certain pollutions in specific areas and specific pollution conditions. This environmental management system adopts comprehensive and moderate-scale control measures to achieve the best environmental, economic and social benefits.
6 Environmental protection target responsibility: This is an administrative system that specifically implements environmental quality maintenance responsibilities to local governments and responsible persons of relevant pollutant discharge units.

China's economic incentive environmental policy tools include the following:

1 Sewage charging system: The fees that emitters who directly or indirectly discharge pollutants to the environment should pay to the government or agency according to the quantity and type of pollutants discharged.
2 Emissions trading system: This method stipulates that the total amount of pollutants discharged within a certain period of time is determined according to the environmental quality requirements of the region in a specific region. On this basis, the government allocates pollutant discharge indicators through licensing and allows indicators to trade on the market.
3 Environmental pollution liability insurance: The polluters of insurance companies collect a deposit for possible damage to the environment. When a polluter has caused a pollution accident due to an accident, the corresponding economic compensation and treatment costs will be borne by the insurance company.
4 Subsidies: These include various types of financial assistance to encourage pollution reduction.

Finally, China's public participation environmental policy tools include the following:

1 Environmental information disclosure: Information disclosure means that managers publish environmental information according to certain rules, such as pollution accident notifications, national or regional environmental status reports and the possible impact of pollution on human health.

30 *Industrial development and policy*

2   Environmental labeling system: As people's environmental awareness is increasingly awakened, more and more consumers prefer environmentally friendly products. In order to distinguish such products from other similar products, environmental labeling systems were designed.
3   ISO14000 environmental series standard: It is the series of environmental management standards that the International Organization for Standardization is responsible for. It includes many environmental issues, such as environmental management system, environmental audit, environmental labeling, life cycle analysis, etc. It aims to guide all types of organizations and companies to implement correct environmental behaviors (Yang, 2009).

3.3.2 Changes in China's environmental policy tools

China's environmental policy tools have undergone a four-year transition process, with the following characteristics in terms of types, legislative orientations and modes of action:

1   The types of environmental policy tools have changed from simple majority to complex diversity. Over the past 40 years of reform and opening up, China has shifted from use of a single command-control–oriented environmental policy tool to a tool system that combines command-control tools, economic incentive tools and public participation tools. It can be said that China's current environmental policy tools have become more and more abundant.
2   The legislative orientation of environmental policy tools has gradually moved from "obligation standard" to "standard of right". The command-control means is characterized by requiring the object under its control to comply with its mandatory requirements. And there is no optional freedom, which is the main feature of obligation fulfillment. The market-based approach has begun to emphasize the right of enterprises to discharge pollutants. Enterprises have begun to have the freedom to choose emissions trading, which is the performance of rights. As for mutual communication, public participation in environmental protection is emphasized. Public participation in environmental protection is not only an extension of democratic thinking in the field of environmental resource protection, but also the basis of the concept of sustainable development.
3   The mode of action of environmental policy instruments has changed from direct government regulation to indirect regulation. In the development of a series of environmental policies such as "standard control – sewage charges – emission permits trading system – environmental labeling", the

Industrial development and policy 31

government's regulatory functions have been continuously reduced, and the government has been transformed from a promoter of environmental policy to a leader of environmental policy. At the same time, enterprises are gradually transformed from passive recipients of environmental policies into active participants in environmental policies.

(Yang, 2009)

3.4 Differential development and differentiated environmental policy

The different environmental pollution conditions in different regions of China has challenged China's environmental protection work in the new era. There is broad consensus that the traditional "one-size-fits-all" environmental management cannot meet the requirements for environmental protection in China. In fact, China's environmental policy has continuously shifted toward regional differentiation. During the 11th Five-Year Plan period, China officially included the "classification guidance" principle in environmental management work. At the same time, the 11th Five-Year Plan of National Environmental Protection put forward the basic principle of "classification guidance, highlighting key points"; that is, "adjusting measures to local conditions, zoning planning, and improve the environmental quality of key river basins, regions, sea areas and cities". During the 12th Five-Year Plan period, it was further clarified that "different environmental policies should be implemented in different regions and industries, and more effective environmental protection measures should be encouraged in areas where conditions permit" The 13th Five-Year Plan of National Environmental Protection proposes to establish a complete management system with clear responsibilities and regulations, effective supervision, implementation of differentiated management, divisional classification and control, grading and sub-item policy and upgrading of refined management. After the 19th National Congress of the Communist Party of China, the construction of ecological civilization in China has been steadily advanced. The concept of environmental protection has been gradually improved, and the working methods have become more precise and effective. With the successive promulgation of the Action Plan for Prevention and Control of Atmospheric Pollution, the Action Plan for Prevention and Control of Water Pollution and the Action Plan for Prevention and Control of Soil Pollution, China's environmental protection work has also turned to the characteristics of zoning and classification to implement more precise environmental management (Liu & Li, 2018).

Different provinces and regions have formulated different environmental policies according to their own economic and social development stages,

32 Industrial development and policy

historical conditions, geographical location and environmental protection needs. Regional differential management has been extended to the fields of air, water, soil and other environmental fields. Environmental policies also show the characteristics of regional differentiation within the same province. For example, air pollution control formulates policies for "2+26 cities", and water pollution control formulates policies according to river basin control units. It can be seen that many environmental regulation differences have been refined to the county (district) level.

Being more specific, first, the environmental levy standards vary from region to region. The environmental tax collection standard is basically the same as the previous sewage charge collection standard, which stipulates that air pollutants should be levied 1.2–12 yuan per pollution equivalent and that water pollutants should be levied 1.4–14 yuan per pollution equivalent. According to the specific needs of environmental protection and regional development, local governments have issued their own environmental tax collection standards within that scope. The applicable tax amount of Beijing taxable air pollutants is 12 yuan per pollution equivalent and the applicable tax amount of taxable water pollutants is 14 yuan per pollution equivalent, which is the highest value set by the state (Liu & Li, 2018). Comparing the latest environmental protection tax levies published by various provinces and regions, the regional differences are obvious. According to the levy standard, the most severe provinces are Beijing, Hebei, Shanghai, Tianjin, Henan, Jiangsu, Shandong and Chongqing, followed by Hunan, Hubei, Shanxi, Guangdong, Guangxi, Sichuan, Guizhou, Hainan and Yunnan. Other provinces are basically levied according to national minimum standards. The residents in the Beijing, Tianjin and Hebei region have increasingly urgent needs for environmental protection, and higher requirements have been placed on environmental tax collection due to the continuous increase in environmental pressure.

Second, different areas have different pollutant discharge standards. In recent years, in order to meet the needs of environmental protection and coordinated economic development in various provinces and regions, local standards on the basis of national standards for pollutant discharge have been put forward in every province according to their actual conditions. According to Liu and Li (2018), 206 provincial and local environmental standards had been registered by the Ministry of Environmental Protection as of April 2017, including 49 in Beijing, 23 in Shanghai, 21 in Shandong, 17 in Hebei, 16 in Guangdong and Chongqing, 13 in Henan, 9 in Tianjin and Zhejiang, etc (Liu & Li, 2018). There are 128 local environmental standards in the Beijing–Tianjin–Hebei area, the Yangtze River Delta and the Pearl River Delta regions, accounting for more than 60% of the national total. At the same time, the state stipulates the implementation of special emission limits for atmospheric pollutants in six major industries, including thermal power, steel, petrochemical, cement, nonferrous metals, chemical industries, and coal-fired boiler projects in key control areas. It involved 47 cities, including the Beijing–Tianjin–Hebei region, the Yangtze River Delta, the Pearl River Delta, etc. In 2018, China decided to implement special emission limits for atmospheric pollutants in the air pollution transmission channel cities in Beijing, Tianjin and Hebei city ("2+26" city). The special emission limits of boiler air pollutants are 20–30 mg/m^3 particulate matter, 50–200 mg/m^3 sulfur dioxide and 150–200 mg/m^3 nitrogen oxide, which are more stringent than the normal national standards. In addition, the country has implemented special discharge limits for water pollutants in the Lake Tai since 2008. In 2014, Zhejiang Province implemented the national emission standard water pollutant discharge limit for 11 industries in the Qiantang River Basin, including pulp and paper, electroplating, down, synthetic leather and artificial leather. An analysis of pollutant discharge standards shows that a large number of local environmental protection standards have been promulgated in the Beijing–Tianjin–Hebei region, the Yangtze River Delta and the Pearl River Delta that are significantly stricter than the national emission standards. With the implementation of special emission limits for atmospheric pollutants in 47 cities in the key control areas and "2+26" cities in the Beijing–Tianjin–Hebei area and the special discharge limits for water pollutants in Lake Tai and the Qiantang River Basin, the regulatory differences in pollutant emission standards among different regions have been strengthened. The "divisional policy" has become more precise. It has been developed by the previous provincial units to the regional units of the city and district (Liu & Li, 2018).

Third, industrial environment access policies vary from region to region. In 2016, four ministries and commissions, including the Ministry of Environmental Protection, jointly issued the *Guidance on Implementation of Action Plan for Water Pollution Prevention and Implementation of Regional Differentiated Environmental Access* and guided the implementation of the *Action Plan for Prevention and Control of Water Pollution*. They put forward guidance on how to implement the strict environmental access requirements in the *Water Pollution Prevention Action Plan* and guide local implementation of differentiated environmental access policies based on watershed water quality objectives and main functional zone planning requirements. Industrial environmental access policy is considered to be an effective means to strengthen source control. The Chinese government is gradually using industrial environmental access policy tools to implement differentiated environmental regulations for different functional areas, and local governments are also actively promoting the formulation of negative lists of industrial access in key ecological functional areas. The industrial environment access policy will have a more direct impact on the regional transfer of related polluting industries. Some regions in China have announced some negative lists of industrial environmental access from the perspective of rationally optimizing their development layout, controlling the intensity of regional development, guiding and restricting various development activities, promoting industrial restructuring and improving the level of industrial greening. For example, Nanjing Municipality stipulates that it is not allowed to build (expand) coal-fired power generation, crude oil processing, steel, cement, polysilicon smelting, flat glass, nonferrous metal smelting and coal-based projects within the city. Examination of environmental tax collection standards, pollutant discharge standards and industrial environmental access policies demonstrates that the environmental regulation levels of different provinces and regions are quite different. On the one hand, the regional differences in the latest environmental protection tax collection standards published by provinces and regions are obvious. The provinces and regions with the highest standards are Beijing, Hebei, Shanghai, Tianjin, Chongqing, Henan and Jiangsu. The Beijing–Tianjin–Hebei, Yangtze River Delta and Pearl River Delta regions have promulgated a large number of local environmental protection standards, all of which are significantly stricter than national emission standards. With the implementation of special emission limits for air pollutants in 47 cities in key control areas and "2+26" cities in the Beijing–Tianjin–Hebei region and special discharge limits for water pollutants in Lake Tai and the Qiantang River Basin, key pollution control areas show increasing regulatory differences in pollutant discharge standards. Provincial governments are gradually using industrial environmental access policy tools to implement differentiated environmental regulations for different functional areas according to the main functional zoning. As a result, environmental regulation levels in highly developed areas such as Beijing, Shanghai, Tianjin, Guangdong, Jiangsu and Zhejiang are relatively high, and the environmental regulation levels in the less developed provinces such as Ningxia, Xinjiang, Gansu, Shanxi and Qinghai are relatively low.

China is a country with a vast territory, and different Chinese regions are at different stages of development. In fact, polluting industries are gradually moving from the east to the central and western regions, which will not only threaten the ecological environment in the central and western regions, but also weaken efforts made by the eastern region in environmental protection and result in the phenomenon of "pollution shelters". Therefore, in the process of undertaking industrial transfer in the eastern region, the central and western regions should also pay attention to the "divisional policy" when laying out polluting industries within the province. It is necessary to protect key ecological functional areas and areas that are ecologically fragile. At the same time, in order to promote the coordinated development of the regional economy and environmental protection, the provinces should give serious consideration to the advantages of environmental capacity and resource carrying capacity of the province, increase industrial concentration, and improve industrial supporting facilities and environmental protection systems (Liu & Li, 2018).

4 Environmental governance and sustainable development

Over the 40 years of reform and opening up, China has experienced rapid industrialization and urbanization and has transitioned from a low-income country to a middle-income country. Over this period, China's environmental governance has been constantly moving forward in twists and turns. From the perspective of the process of pollution control and emission reduction, China has generally repeated the development path of "first pollution and then governance" that developed countries have generally passed and has now crossed the "environmental inflection point". From the perspective of system construction, China's environmental protection legislation, organizational system, policy system, supervision method, responsibility system and accountability mechanism have undergone profound changes. The governance system of multi-participation has been basically formed, and the environmental governance system is constantly improving (Chen, 2018).

China's environmental governance has improved tremendously despite a number of constraints, but environmental problems are still serious. One of the reasons for this is that local governments and environmental management departments have many imperfections in the implementation of environmental policies. Environmental policy implementation faces a series of difficulties and challenges. Therefore, implementation of environmental policies by local governments must be strengthened to improve environmental governance. An analysis and discussion of the implementation of environmental policies by local governments in China can help to solve the dilemma.

4.1 The effectiveness of China's environmental governance

In recent years (especially since the 11th Five-Year Plan), under the guidance of building ecological civilization and exploring new avenues of environmental protection, and under the constraints of various environmental policies, China's environmental protection has realized important changes from its implementation practice.

First, the total amount of pollutants discharged has continued to decline dramatically, and significant progress has been made in environmental governance. China regards energy conservation and emission reduction as a guiding indicator for economic and social development planning. By strengthening the target responsibility assessment, paying close attention to project emission reduction, structural emission reduction and management emission reduction, the national urban sewage treatment rate has increased from 52% in 2005 to 85% in 2012. At the same time, the proportion of desulfurization units in coal-fired power plants has increased from 14% to 90%. During the 11th Five-Year Plan period, emissions of sulfur dioxide and chemical oxygen demand decreased by 14.29% and 12.45%, respectively (Zhou, 2013). As a result, the quality of the main river water environment gradually improved. In 2014, the total amount of five major heavy metal pollutants (lead, mercury, cadmium, chromium and metalloids) in the country decreased by one-fifth compared with 2007. Heavy metal pollution incidents decreased from more than 10 in 2010–2011 to an average of 3 in 2012–2014 (Cao, 2015). In addition, the "Blue Sky Protection Campaign" has made great achievements. By 2017, the average concentration of PM10 in 338 prefecture-level cities had decreased by 22.7% since 2013. Over the same period, the average concentration of PM2.5 in the Beijing–Tianjin–Hebei region, the Yangtze River Delta and the Pearl River Delta decreased by 39.6%, 34.3% and 27.7%, respectively. The average concentration of PM2.5 in Beijing decreased from 89.5 μg/m^3 in 2013 to 58 μg/m^3 in 2017. The air quality improvement target and key tasks of the *Action Plan for Prevention and Control of Atmospheric Pollution* were fully completed (Bulletin of China's Ecological Environment, 2017).

Second, the protection of the ecological environment has been strengthened. In terms of afforestation and greening, China has vigorously carried out afforestation work over the years so that the forest area and forest stocks have increased rapidly. The forest-age structure and forest-phase structure have become more reasonable, and forest quality has tended to improve, achieving a historic turning of continuous decline to gradual increase (Yang, 2009). At present, the national forest area is 208 million hectares, and the forest coverage rate is 21.63%. Forest reserves are 15.137 billion cubic meters. According to the results of the Global Forest Resources Assessment 2015 released by the Food and Agriculture Organization of the United Nations, China's forest area and forest accumulation rank fifth and sixth, respectively, in the world, and the area of planted forests ranks first in the world (Bulletin of China's Ecological Environment,

2017). By the end of 2012, 363 national nature reserves had been built nationwide. Fifteen provinces (districts and municipalities) had carried out ecological province construction. More than 1000 counties (cities and districts) had carried out ecological county construction. At the same time, 53 areas carried out pilot work on ecological civilization construction. In 2017, the State Council approved the establishment of 17 new national nature reserves, bringing the total to 463 (Zhou, et al, 2018).

Third, the quality of the urban environment has improved. Urbanization is an irreversible trend in China's economic and social development process. The urbanization rate increased from 36% in 2000 to 57.96% in 2017, and it will continue to increase into the future. Governments at all levels have taken a series of comprehensive measures to deal with the environmental problems arising from urbanization, thus the environmental quality of cities has improved. In 2000, 36.5% of monitored cities reached the second level of air quality, increasing to 56.1% in 2005 and 74.3% in 2017. This indicates that the air quality of Chinese cities is improving. The national urban sewage treatment rate was 46% in 2004, but by 2017 the national urban sewage treatment capacity reached 157 million cubic meters per day and the national urban sewage treatment rate exceeded 80%. By the end of 2017, the national domestic garbage removal volume reached 215,497,700 tons. The harmless treatment capacity was 638,208 tons per day and the harmless treatment capacity was 20,931,100 tons. The harmless treatment rate of urban domestic garbage reached 97.14%, nearly double that of 52% in 2004 (Bulletin of China's Ecological Environment, 2017).

In general, emissions of pollutants in China have generally peaked, and environmental quality has entered a stable and positive phase. Looking back at the history of environmental governance since reform and opening up, it can be roughly divided into two stages. In the first stage, during the 30 years of rapid industrialization, pollution emissions in China increased greatly and overall environmental quality deteriorated. In the second stage, from the 11th Five-Year Plan and 12th Five-Year Plan period, the rapid increase in the total discharge of major pollutants in China was curbed. Today, the discharge of major pollutants has peaked or entered a "platform period". According to the analytical framework of the "environmental Kuznets curve", and compared with the process of environmental improvement in developed countries, China has crossed the "environmental inflection point" and the overall quality of the environment has entered a stable and better stage. From the perspective of international comparison, China's per capita GDP was lower when major pollution emissions reached their peak compared with other countries (Chen, 2018).

4.2 Policy defects and implications for sustainable development

Since reform and opening up, the Chinese government has done a lot of work on environmental protection and has achieved some successes. However, it must be pointed out that the Chinese government still faces challenges in environmental governance. The grim situation of China's environmental situation has not been totally reversed. The defects in China's environmental governance can be traced to problems with its environmental policies, such as multiple political policies and unclear rights and responsibilities, deviations in environmental policy implementation, lack of continuity in environmental policy implementation, insufficient interaction of environmental policy supervisors and low efficiency of environmental policy tools. These problems are then exacerbated by the lack of coordination among the formulators, the lack of consistency in environmental policy implementation, the imperfect environmental assessment system, the imperfect environmental policy supervision mechanism and the insufficient selectivity of environmental policy tools. In order to truly improve China's environmental conditions, the government must start with the formulation of sound environmental policies. The deviations in the implementation of environmental policies should be resolved, environmental policy tools should be improved and environmental policy evaluation systems and monitoring mechanisms should be established.

4.2.1 Multiple political policies and unclear rights and responsibilities

Through an examination of China's environmental policy, we find that environmental policy formulation in China involves more than 30 government departments having various scopes. Multi-sectoral participation does not necessarily have a positive cooperative effect. The main body of environmental policy formulation in China is the Ministry of Environmental Protection; other departments have not assumed as many environmental protection responsibilities. However, each of these departments has its own policy objectives. Inevitably, these objectives may conflict, which will affect the overall cooperation of the various departments with regards to environmental policies (Zhong, 2016).

4.2.2 Deviations in environmental policy implementation

With regard to environmental governance, the central government pays great attention to environmental issues and sets ambitious environmental goals, which contradicts the local government's emphasis on the economy and neglect of the environment. Although the new Environmental Protection Law incorporates environmental protection into the local government assessment system, it has encountered tremendous resistance in the implementation process. Implementation of environmental policies in China still faces difficulties, mainly in the following aspects.

First, the division of power and responsibility between central and local governments is not clear. There is no clear definition of the environmental responsibility of the central government in China's current environmental governance system. On the one hand, the central government holds too much authority for environmental management, which often leads to the phenomenon of functional offside. For example, the central government has invested limited manpower, financial resources and material resources into the specific work of pollution control of rivers or lakes and inspection of corporate discharge standards, which has caused excessive interference in local environmental management details. On the other hand, the central government's coordination and management of environmental management across administrative regions is not good enough, which result in a lack of a unified and effective coordination mechanism between administrative regions. For example, regional environmental problems such as haze, acid rain and acid deposition caused by emission of pollutants are difficult to address across administrative boundaries. Without the effective unified dispatch of central government, the local governments are unable to coordinate and govern.

Second, some local governments have distorted the implementation of environmental policies. Local governments are the actual implementers of environmental policies. Under the background that the central government has been assessing local officials with economic development indicators for a long time, local governments often distort and choose to implement environmental policies or even set obstacles to environmental management rights exercised by environmental protection departments driven by the pursuit of economic interests. The Ministry of Environmental Protection is specifically responsible for the implementation of environmental policies, but it's under the dual leadership of local governments and higher-level environmental protection departments. Due to the dual pressures of funds and administration of local government, it is difficult for local environmental protection agencies to fulfill their responsibilities.

Finally, the authority of the environmental management department is misplaced and overlapping. The problems of decentralized allocation of environmental management functions, cross-cutting of institutional settings and unclear responsibility are prominent. Different departments compete for management of profitable affairs, while passing the buck on difficult environmental matters. The comprehensive control ability of the environmental protection department is weak, and the high-level negotiation and coordination mechanism between departments is not perfect. The Ministry of Environmental Protection has been given responsibility for the development and implementation of environmental policies, but it lacks adequate policy tools. Therefore, it is very difficult for the environmental protection department to organize and coordinate the environmental protection work among various departments, and it is difficult for unified supervision to be in place (Han, 2017).

4.2.3 Lack of continuity in environmental policy implementation

The sustainability of an environmental policy is an indicator of its effectiveness. An environmental policy is based on the current set of environmental issues. Whether it can adapt to existing environmental problems and achieve the predetermined policy effect is an important criterion for judging its impact. The realization of the policy's objectives requires flexibility. However, from the perspective of the dynamic process of public policy, China's environmental policy does not have good adaptability in its implementation. From the perspective of policy texts, most environmental policies do not consider the adaptability of policies and the environment. Take China's nature protection policy as an example. China's eco-environmental policy system was mostly established in the 1990s. Due to the influence of the planned economy at that time, the nature protection policy had a strong reliance on planning and guidance. If this type of system continues to guide China's natural environmental protection work, there will be some policies that do not meet the current state of ecological environmental protection in China. Owing to the existence of this situation, environmental policies are out of line with the internal and external environment. Therefore, although many environmental policies have been formulated by government departments, there are still some problems such as unsatisfactory synergistic effect of environmental policies and insufficient effect of environmental supervision due to the inadaptability of environmental policies to the external socio-economic environment that causes environmental problems.

4.2.4 Insufficient interaction of environmental policy supervisors

Policy supervision guarantees the orderly operation of the policy system. Therefore, it is necessary to establish an environmental policy supervision system. According to policy analysis, the environmental policy promulgation department of China is responsible for the supervision of environmental policy implementation. Thirty-one functional departments, including the Ministry of Environmental Protection, the Ministry of Finance and the Ministry of Commerce, are responsible for policy supervision. In addition, there is also public supervision. The pluralistic supervisory bodies have formed a relatively complete supervision system, but many supervisory bodies do not coordinate well. Some supervisory bodies shirked their responsibilities, which led to the emergence of "empty supervision".

4.2.5 Low efficiency of environmental policy tools

The complex external environment that causes environmental problems requires the use of a variety of environmental policy tools. Only in this way can the coordination effect be diverse. To quote the welfare effect of economics, the synergistic effect of policy instruments may bring about either positive or negative external effects. If it is a positive external effect, it means that the environmental policy tools have had their due policy effects of solving policy problems and achieving policy goals. In contrast, if it is a negative external effect, it will weaken the implementation of policy tools. Although there is a strong correlation among various environmental policy instruments in China, this kind of synergy is more negative coordination. China's environmental supervision has made great achievements, but it is undeniable that China's environmental problems have not been fundamentally improved while more and more environmental policies have been issued. The reality is a good testimony to the poor coordination among environmental policy tools, which leads to insufficient environmental supervision (Zhong, 2016).

4.3 Policy issues and sustainable development

4.3.1 "Fragmentation" and the lack of coordination among the formulators

"Fragmentation" is an apt description of the current administrative organization in China, which is manifested as "unclear powers and responsibilities, multiple political affairs and overlapping duties". It can be more vividly described as the "structural gap" among "fragments". This gap is the manifestation of the fragmentation operation mechanism at the level of government structure, and it is the "political gap" in the government process. This kind of governance creates gaps in responsibility.

First, the effect of this "fragmentation" on environmental policy is manifested as conflicts of interest among the various policy makers. This leads to competition between government departments that have similar interests.

Typically, various government departments compete for limited resources; they all want a share of the same pie. In contrast, in areas where there is less interest or no profit, there is a situation of mutual shirking and dereliction of duty. In addition, there is a lack of cooperation mechanisms between the various departments. The "fragmented" organizational structure emphasizes the division of labor, while the horizontal inter-departmental structure is loose and the correlation is not strong. This has led to the neglect of macro-coordination and cooperation among departments.

Second, the high cost of cooperation among departments leads to a weak sense of cooperation. With the expansion of government functions, the transformation of economies of scale on the basis of specialized division of labor has become a new way to improve the efficiency of government organizations. The implementation of the new approach needs to be based on continuous collaboration among departments. Inter-governmental cooperation requires the sharing of information and complementary resources, as well as some regulatory costs in order to ensure the progress of collaboration. All these constitute a cost of inter-departmental coordination. However, the departments are still deeply affected by the division of workers in the real political life. Exercising their powers in their own fields, they neglect the interdependence and complementarity between each other. As a result, coordination costs are too high, which in turn constrains inter-departmental cooperation.

Finally, resource monopoly leads to the loose structure between horizontal sectors and the lack of cooperation mechanisms. Government departments have the key information resources needed for decision-making, but the increasing complexity of social issues requires more specialized decision-making. Therefore, sector experts in specialized fields play an increasingly important role in decision-making. Environmental regulation covers a wide range of issues, including environmental prevention and post-event management. In this process, both production control policies and financial support are needed. However, in view of China's current environmental policies, policy formulation is still dominated by the Ministry of Environmental Protection. As the leading department of environmental policy, the Ministry of Environmental Protection lacks production support and related financial experts, which will inevitably lead to the lack of professional guidance. This weakens the effects of the policies.

4.3.2 The lack of consistency in environmental policy implementation

First, the negative impact of the interest-driven mechanism results in a lack of consistency in the implementation of environmental policy. Sometimes there is a conflict of interest between policy makers and those implementing a policy. Most of China's environmental policies are formulated by the central government and then implemented by local governments, which is a decentralized process. At present, the current situation of government performance appraisal based on GDP has not changed greatly. In fact, environmental policies will restrict the development of the local economy to a large extent. This often results in the phenomenon of "the government has its policies and people down below have their own ways of getting around them". In some cases, local governments only carry out environmental policies on the surface, without actual action, resulting in a significant reduction in the effectiveness of environmental policies. On the other hand, there is a game of competing interests in the process of environmental governance. The central government is responsible for setting environmental policy and is the first actor in policy implementation. The central government's responsibility for the governance environment cannot be transferred to others. Therefore, the most stringent policies must be adopted to deal with environmental issues. As decentralized policy executors, the local executors have the power to formulate local policies and can transfer environmental responsibilities. When central policies jeopardize their interests, they will weaken the effectiveness of policy implementation. In addition, there is a game of interests between companies and policies. When the policy can improve the performance of enterprises, enterprises will actively support it. On the contrary, when the policy damages the performance of enterprises, they will look for various policy loopholes and even carry out corporate activities in violation of the policy. The game between government and enterprises is more obvious because of the asymmetry of information.

Second, the lack of communication among policy executives has led to the lack of consistency in environmental policy implementation. It is undeniable that everyone is responsible for environmental protection. However, environmental protection in China should have an important executive body, the government. From the perspective of the central government, the highest executive body of China's environmental policy is the Ministry of Environmental Protection. Its responsibilities involve various aspects related to the environment. The most important thing is to protect the ecological environment and control pollution. At the same time, it formulates environmental protection policies and guidelines from a macro perspective and supervises and coordinates the implementation of policies. Various departments strictly implement policies according to this level. The committee on environment and resources protection related to environmental protection in the National People's Congress is responsible for legislation and supervision of implementation. The local governments are responsible for environmental protection legislation and planning within their local jurisdictions. The provincial and municipal first-level environmental protection bureaus are mainly responsible for environmental protection and implementation of relevant environmental protection laws or national environmental protection policies within the jurisdiction. They also supervise and control local environmental pollution. Although we have a relatively complete environmental protection department, the emergence of environmental problems is caused by multiple factors, not a single factor. There is over-detailed division of functions and overlapping responsibilities among departments. When there is a problem, if it is in their own interest to solve them they will compete for management, but when it is harmful to their interests they will pass the buck. Therefore, cooperation between departments is very difficult. In addition, since China's environmental policies are mostly implemented by different localities, regionalization of environmental governance has emerged. In fact, environmental protection has no regional boundaries. The public nature of environmental protection leads to the transfer of responsibility for protection.

Third, the lack of supporting mechanisms for environmental policies has led to a lack of consistency in environmental policy implementation. The implementation of the policy will ultimately be implemented by individuals. People have different needs. In order to meet their own needs, they will distort the original policies to varying degrees. The current personnel assessment mechanism in China has provided conditions for this behavior. China's current government assessment mechanism is mostly based on monetary-based economic development indicators. In pursuit of promotion and political achievements, government personnel usually only value economic development while ignoring environmental and resource protection. According to the experience of environmental management in developed countries, we can find that public participation in environmental protection work in China is not successful because this directive-type environmental protection method does not mobilize the enthusiasm of public participation. It can be seen that the imperfect mechanism of public participation, the absence of a platform for public participation, the lack of satisfaction and feedback of environmental protection and the high cost of obtaining environmental protection information all weaken the enthusiasm of public participation. On the other hand, the avenues for public participation are very limited. There is a lack of supervision over policy implementation. At the same time, China's current environmental policies mostly exist in the form of advice, notification, planning, methods and other policies with relatively low intensity at the macro-level, with few existing in the form of laws and regulations. This shows that China's governance of environmental issues mostly points out the direction of governance from a macro perspective rather than mandatory management through law. As a result, relevant personnel do not have to bear the consequences of not implementing environmental policies, which leads to the weakening of policy effects.

4.3.3 The imperfect environmental policy assessment system

The process of environmental policy assessment and feedback is that the assessment entity collects relevant information in the process of environmental policy formulation and implementation through various means and analyzes the information to determine whether the environmental policy meets the expected goals. Then they feed back the results of the assessment to the policy makers to propose countermeasures and recommendations that contribute to the effective functioning of the environmental policy. Policy evaluation provides feedback in the process of policy formulation and implementation to policy makers, thus continuously improving the quality and efficiency of policies. At the same time, it can avoid policy deviations from objectives to a large extent. Policy evaluation enables policy content and direction to be constantly adjusted according to policy issues, which can greatly enhance policy credibility and improve the guiding role of policy. It can be concluded that China's environmental policy has not fully played its due role through the process of environmental policy assessment and feedback. Why is this the case? Although the Chinese government pays more and more attention to the status of policy evaluation and feedback in the policy process, it has not formed a normative system. For example, policy evaluation is still dominated by policy makers, and there is a lack of external participation in policy evaluation. Policy makers evaluate themselves, leading to the failure to identify problems in the process of environmental policy. Or, if there is external participation in policy assessments, the results are not taken seriously. This will lead to the inconsistency of the operational systems of environmental policy.

4.3.4 The imperfect environmental policy supervision mechanism

In China's environmental supervision system, there is a lack of cooperation and communication between the various supervisory bodies, and an effective overall system cannot be formed. There is no effective coordination among various supervisory mechanisms, resulting in numerous gaps. For example, when different administrative organizations have diverging objectives, there is no effective coordination and guidance mechanism. At the same time, supervision lacks institutionalized norms. It only gives authority to the policy subjects, public opinion and public supervision. However, there are no corresponding provisions on what to supervise, how to supervise or how to deal with the results of supervision. Therefore, in the event of environmental problems, the supervisory bodies shirk their responsibilities and conflicts continue. Another reason for this "empty supervision" is the lack of information communication mechanisms among the supervisory bodies. Information asymmetry is a serious problem with environmental policy issues. Due to the different degree of information among different supervisors, it is easy for the supervisors to subjectively believe that the supervisory responsibility has been assumed by other subjects or nobody else. However, the opposite is true, which results in lack of supervision or duplicate supervision.

4.3.5 Insufficient selectivity of environmental policy tools

Although the types of environmental policy tools in China have changed from simple to complex, most of them are still dominated by regulatory policy tools. Although there are also guiding policy tools, the proportion is relatively small. This phenomenon has weakened the effectiveness of China's environmental policy.

First, although the effect of regulatory policy tools is relatively ideal, they require information symmetry. Regulatory policy tools require governments to effectively collect information about environmental issues. When information asymmetry occurs, policy failures occur. Consider the three simultaneous systems as an example. As a regulatory policy tool, it can force enterprises to invest in environmental protection, but it does not bring economic benefits to enterprises. Thus, enterprises will use information asymmetry to avoid institutional regulations, resulting in unsatisfactory policy effects. Second, from the perspective of China's current guiding environmental protection policy tools, policy tools have not been widely promoted except for the sewage charging system. The sewage charging system has indeed played a great role in environmental protection, but there are still many problems, such as unreasonable charging standards, lack of geographical differentiation and poor flexibility. Moreover, we can find that the functions of some policy tools are not unified with the original design intention. For example, sewage charges should be an incentive for corporate environmental protection, but it has more often become a tool for raising funds. The same problem exists with environmental taxes. The legal status of environmental taxes is not clear and does not directly reflect the protection of the environment. Guiding policy tools lack the incentive effect that they should have, and they need to be further enriched and improved. Finally, environmental protection policy tools ignore the application of public participation other than government and enterprises. According to the environmental policies issued by China in recent years, public participation is mainly reflected in education and publicity, as well as the publication of environmental bulletins. In China, the government still plays a leading role, and the public has not really participated in environmental protection (Zhong, 2016).

4.4 Countermeasures for the implementation of environmental policy

The reasons for the dilemma of China's environmental policy implementation are very complicated, and the impacts and consequences of policy failures cannot be overstated. Therefore, it is necessary to resolve the dilemma of China's environmental policy implementation. According to the above-mentioned reasons for the failure of effective implementation of environmental policy, we believe that the following could play a role in resolving the dilemma of China's environmental policy implementation.

4.4.1 Promoting institutional innovation

1 China should clarify the central and local environmental protection responsibilities and achieve positive interactions. On the one hand, at the central level, the Ministry of Environmental Protection should be the mainstay to establish an integrated and comprehensive environmental management system across departments and regions. A special Environmental Protection Commission under the State Council should be established to guide and coordinate the environmental protection responsibilities, objectives and tasks of various departments, as well as to guide and coordinate the work of ecological protection and pollution prevention in inter-provincial areas and river basins. At the same time, it is necessary to reward and punish the environmental performance of various departments of the State Council and local governments. It is of great importance to strengthen the authority of the Ministry of Environmental Protection and its ability to control local environmental protection. On the other hand, at the local level, it should be guided by the county. The environmental protection bureaus of the provinces, autonomous regions, and municipalities directly under the Central Government should be responsible for the environmental management within the jurisdiction. It is necessary to reduce the levels of management and strengthen administrative supervision. An effective environmental accountability system should also be established and the improvement of environmental quality should be regarded as a hard indicator of the performance evaluation of local governments during their term of office. Third parties should be regularly organized to evaluate the

performance of the relevant ministries and commissions of the State Council and local governments, and publicly evaluate the results. If necessary, a one-vote veto system should be required to ensure that local economic development meets the local and national environmental protection objectives.

2 It is important to transform the government's environmental management functions to achieve a transition to an eco-government. In terms of functional scope, the Chinese government should shift from an omnipotent government to a government that only provides environmental public services and environmental public goods. In terms of functional focus, the Chinese government should shift from merely regulating industry and enterprises to dual supervision of enterprises and the government itself, and shifting from adapting to economic development to optimizing economic development through environmental protection; in terms of government functions and means, the Chinese government should shift from relying on command-control means to adopting comprehensive means such as administrative compulsory, administrative guidance, market incentives, as well as soft, flexible and humane government functions. In order to play the role of ecological government, it is necessary to establish a set of assessment system with the green performance evaluation standard as the core to standardize and guide the environmental governance behavior of cadres. What is more, the Chinese government should not only incorporate hard indicators such as green GDP, energy conservation and emission reduction into local government assessment, but also establish an environmental management evaluation benchmark in performance evaluation. It is important to change the local government's view of political achievements to suppress and regulate the environmental pollution speculation of local governments and enterprises. Alienation in environmental enforcement should also be reduced. The strengthening of local government environmental awareness, environmental literacy and environmental governance is the key to achieving environmental policy goals.

3 It is necessary to establish an inter-ministerial coordination mechanism to enhance the coordination and implementation capabilities of the Ministry of Environmental Protection. A Leading Group of Ecological Civilization Construction should be established to supervise and coordinate environmental strategies, environmental quality and other related work. They should also provide environmental policy advice for central decision-making. The leading group should be led by a member of the State Council leadership with the heads of various departments as its members. The office should be located in the Ministry of Environmental Protection. The Leading Group of Ecological Civilization

Construction should become the leading agency for coordinating the ministries and commissions of the State Council on environmental protection and ecological construction. In particular, it should coordinate the relationship between the Ministry of Environmental Protection, the comprehensive economic decision-making departments, resource management departments and other departments so as to solve the problems involved with horizontal coordination with regards to environmental policy. In addition, the reform of the system of "larger government departments" for environmental protection should be carried out. The main environmental protection functions scattered among the relevant ministries and commissions of the state should be centralized in the Ministry of Environmental Protection to form a unified coordination and management structure of the Ministry of Environmental Protection, as well as other comprehensive coordination mechanisms based on supervision by relevant ministries.

4.4.2 Improving the mechanism of environmental policies

1 China should strengthen economic means and build a mature market regulation mechanism. First, it is necessary to clarify the definition of property rights of environmental resources and to promote the reform of pricing mechanisms for key resources such as water resources, electricity, coal, oil and natural gas. An environmental resource cost pricing mechanism based on the market and reflecting resource scarcity should be constructed to enable the economic actors involved in the market to internalize resource and environmental costs spontaneously. Second, ecological compensation must be promoted in key river basins and ecological functional areas. Emissions fees should be fully levied. What's more, the relevant stakeholders should adjust the relationship between the distribution of environmental benefits and economic benefits. Third, the Chinese government should implement guided classification policies. The government should promote voluntary environmental action of enterprises at different levels and implement incentive preferential policies. The government should also guide enterprises to vigorously carry out economic activities such as low-carbon economy, circular economy, environmental protection industry and green trade.

2 China should reform its fiscal and taxation policies and create incentives and restraint mechanisms for energy conservation and emission reduction. First, the preferential policy of environmental protection for enterprise income tax should be implemented. Environmental protection projects and environmental protection special equipment catalogues that meet the requirements and enjoy preferential income

tax should be formulated to encourage enterprises to purchase special equipment for environmental protection and control pollution. Second, it is necessary to continue the development of a catalogue of high-pollution and high-environmental risk products and put forward proposals for canceling export tax rebates. A differential tax rate should be implemented instead. New taxes that limit energy consumption and high pollution should be introduced. The government should reduce and stop financial subsidies that have serious negative impacts on resources and the environment. Third, the government should intensify the reform of consumption tax and include some products with serious environmental pollution and large consumption of resources into the scope of consumption tax collection.

3   China should increase capital investment and broaden investment channels for environmental protection. On the one hand, China should improve the environmental public finance system and improve the performance of environmental protection investment. The new financial resources of all levels of government should be inclined to environmental protection investment. The government should gradually increase the proportion of environmental protection investment in the government budget and ensure that the growth rate of environmental public expenditure is higher than the growth rate of GDP and fiscal revenue. On the other hand, relevant market mechanisms should be improved in order to encourage social capital to enter the field of environmental protection. A national environmental protection investment company should be established to issue municipal environmental bonds. The government should make full use of credit, bonds, trust investment and bank loans to raise environmental protection funds through multiple channels. It is also important to build an information communication platform for the environmental protection department and the financial system. Through the platform, cooperation between the environmental protection department and the credit systems can be improved, and the environmental performance index of China's securities market can be compiled and released.

4.4.3 Improving the environmental legal system

1   China should construct a dynamic and comprehensive environmental legislation system. First, the concept of ecological management must be strengthened at the constitutional level. President Xi Jinping pointed out that the establishment of an ecological civilization concept that respects nature, conforms to nature and protects nature is the foundation for promoting the construction of ecological civilization.

Therefore, the legislative spirit of respecting ecology, protecting nature and respecting the living rights of other living species should be established in the constitution, which provides the necessary constitutional basis for the "ecologicalization" of departmental law. Second, the government should strengthen the understanding of the scientific and technological internal causes of environmental law. Many environmental legal norms are technical norms themselves. Environmental legislation must reflect the importance of the internal and technological factors of environmental protection. Environmental protection laws should be updated and their scope broadened based on the most current scientific and technical knowledge. Third, the government should explore the most effective mode of environmental administrative law enforcement and criminal justice. Penalties for environmental violations should be flexible and diverse while focusing on the integrity and coordination of the environmental legal system. It is also important to strengthen judicial safeguards such as civil environmental litigation rights. In a word, the Chinese government should promote the establishment of a systematic, efficient and effective system of environmental rule of law.

2   China should reform the environmental law enforcement supervision mechanism to make the environmental law enforcement supervision achieve the unity of internal supervision and external constraints. On the one hand, a coordinated and orderly internal law enforcement supervision system should be established to ensure internal information exchange and communication coordination. It is also necessary to integrate and optimize the environmental law enforcement supervision functions dispersed in the relevant departments of the State Council and to strengthen the construction of local environmental law enforcement supervision institutions. What is more, paying attention to regional and river basin environmental law enforcement supervision and cooperation as well as forming a mechanism for information sharing, joint inspection and environmental event coordination is of great importance. On the other hand, China should create a coordinated and orderly external constraint environment and build an environmental supervision model of government-led, social coordination and public participation. Environmental management authorities should take the initiative to publicize their power, responsibility and performance status in order to promote the openness and transparency of information on environmental law enforcement supervision. China should improve the reporting system of environmental complaints and establish a system of social environmental supervisors. At the same time, it is also important to improve the environmental hearing system and establish a system of news release of major environmental violations.

3 It is important to strengthen the environmental law enforcement team and improve the effectiveness of environmental law enforcement. First, it is necessary to build a first-line environmental law enforcement supervision team that matches the environmental tasks. Especially in areas with more environmental emergencies and prominent environmental problems, sufficient personnel should be centralized. For example, the establishment of an environmental police team and the promotion of a joint law enforcement model of environmental protection and public security should be explored. In fact, 11 cities in Hebei Province established an Environmental Security Corps in 2013, becoming the first area to set up an environmental police corps in China. Second, China should improve the overall quality of law enforcement personnel. It is necessary to combine the professional quality of law enforcement personnel with training in law enforcement so as to improve their sensitivity to environmental events and their flexibility in dealing with problems. In addition, it is also important to promote the standardization of environmental monitoring, improve the level of environmental law enforcement equipment and ensure that law enforcement hardware facilities are complete (Han, 2017).

4.4.4 Developing environmental technology

1 China should strengthen the support capabilities of environmental protection technology and the environmental protection industry. First, the government should guide enterprises to participate in environmental science and technology innovation and give full play to the main role of corporate environmental protection technology investment to promote the development of environmental engineering technology consulting, environmental protection facilities operation, environmental monitoring and environmental analysis. In addition, the scale of the environmental protection industry should be upgraded to form a pattern of moderate concentration within the industry and full competition as well as coordinated development among enterprises. Second, it is necessary to establish a regional innovation system for environmental science and technology. The government in China should organically combine the central and local scientific and technological forces in order to promote the rational allocation and efficient use of scientific and technological resources. It is also necessary to establish and improve regional innovation systems. China should improve regional scientific and technological innovation capabilities and implement environmental strategies such as the strategy of regional environmental protection technology system construction, the radiation-driven strategy of scientific and

technological innovation in central cities and the cluster innovation strategy. Third, it is important to cultivate and develop various types of science and technology intermediary service organizations. At the same time, the government should guide the science and technology intermediary service organizations to develop in the direction of specialization, scale and standardization.

2   Advanced environmental monitoring and early warning systems should be built. First, the national environmental monitoring network should be optimized and adjusted to monitor and report on the national environmental quality. The state should grasp the national and regional environmental quality situation as well as its changes, and the situation of pollutant emissions. It is necessary to be able to conduct emergency monitoring and effective early warning of environmental emergencies. In addition, China should establish an environmental and health risk assessment mechanism nationwide to strengthen the work of environmental and health risk warning. Second, the government should speed up the construction of provincial- and municipal-level local environmental monitoring networks. This is necessary to meet the requirements of non-overlapping monitoring tasks and to share monitoring data and scientific coverage of the three-level environmental monitoring network. An environmental monitoring network system with representative monitoring data and meeting the requirements of environmental supervision should be established. Third, China should carry out basic research and applied technology research on environmental monitoring to improve the scientific and technological content of an environmental monitoring and early warning system. This also will accelerate the transformation of scientific and technological achievements of environmental monitoring, ultimately strengthening the role of scientific and technological innovation in building an advanced environmental monitoring and early warning system. Finally, the development process of automation, serialization, localization and industrialization of environmental monitoring instruments should be accelerated. In this way, it can lay the foundation for the establishment of an advanced environmental monitoring and early warning system and ensure the long-term, smooth operation of the environmental monitoring and early warning system.

3   China should strengthen the integration and sharing capacity of environmental information. The basic capacity building of an information collection infrastructure and environmental information network should be accelerated, and an "environmental information hub" and environmental information database should be established. Environmental information should be incorporated into the construction of a

key business information system of national e-government projects to promote the sharing and exchange of environmental information resources within and outside the environmental protection system and to ensure the sharing and utilization of environmental information. In addition, environmental and health monitoring data should be properly stored, collected, aggregated, invoked and secured. China should unify environmental and health data codes and be in line with international standards to strengthen data quality control, quality assurance and auditing. Only in this way can China form effective monitoring data information resources, and achieve the goal of providing basic data for environmental and health research and providing a scientific basis for national and local environmental management decisions.

4.4.5 Promoting public participation in environmental protection

1   China should establish an innovative environmental education model to enhance public participation in environmental protection initiatives. China should broaden the environmental protection publicity channels and work hard to form a standardized and systematic citizen environmental education system. On the basis of grasping the citizens' willingness and ability to participate in environmental protection, the government needs to conduct targeted environmental education on people of different educational and knowledge levels. At the same time, it is necessary for China to actively build a national environmental education base to build a broad stage for citizens to participate in environmental protection. The government should try to set up a demonstration environmental education base which integrates exhibition, education and training, cultural exchange, news release and other functions according to the actual development needs of provinces (districts), cities and regions. In this way, China can actively promote the solid establishment and popularization of the concept of ecological civilization among all citizens.

2   China should deepen public participation and improve the environmental supervision system. First, the right of public participation and supervision should be expanded in the process of environmental policy formulation, environmental law enforcement and environmental prediction and assessment to ensure the full participation of the public and prevent the phenomenon of public participation in slogans or "go through the motions". It is necessary to explore the implementation of a round-table dialogue mechanism of community environment and establish a mechanism and platform for regular communication and

equal dialogue among the government, enterprises and the public. Second, the government of China should improve environmental systems such as the legislation of major environmental policies and environmental impact assessment. The legislative hearing procedure needs to be improved, and the democratization of environmental decision-making should be promoted. In addition, China must improve the environmental news publicity and management mechanism so that it plays the role of public opinion guidance and supervision of the news media. Finally, it is of great importance to improve the environmental information release platform, public participation platform and information collection feedback platform to ensure that the public participates in environmental protection practice conveniently, quickly and orderly.

3 China should foster non-governmental environmental protection organizations and create a relaxed and coordinated atmosphere of public participation. First, in terms of management mechanism, the government should "unbind" the associations and create an institutional environment conducive to the development of non-governmental environmental protection organizations. At the same time, non-governmental environmental protection organizations should be given necessary guidance to incorporate citizens' concerns and wishes for environmental affairs into the institutionalized and orderly public participation track. Second, environmental organizations need to clarify their missions and goals and improve their ability to express and safeguard environmental rights. For example, they should actively participate in law enforcement supervision of administrative agencies, promote the development of environmental public interest litigation systems and actively participate in the implementation of environmental management systems (Han, 2017).

The report of the 18th National Congress of the Communist Party of China pointed out that "the protection of the ecological environment must depend on the system", which shows that the formulation, implementation and improvement of the institutional system are the most important parts of the construction of ecological civilization (Hu, 2012). Only by removing the institutional and institutional obstacles that restrict the construction of ecological civilization and putting environmental protection policies into practice can we promote green development and have a beautiful China with clear waters and green mountains.

5 Industrial structure upgrading and environmental regulations in China

Although China's economy is growing rapidly, it is still a developing country and a country with a large population. In fact, improvements in people's living standards, such as daily food, housing, transportation, education, health, medical care and other aspects, rely heavily on economic growth as a foundation. Therefore, while managing the environment and saving resources, China still needs to attach great importance to economic growth and industrial development. Industrial support and sustainable development are the meso-based foundation of a country's continuous economic growth. The upgrading of the industrial structure is an important issue in China's economic transformation and restructuring. Upgrading and optimizing the industrial structure, realizing the steady transformation of China's economic structure, taking the green development path of low pollution and low energy consumption and improving technology and total factor productivity are all starting points for China's industrial development policy and strategic planning, as well as the key factors for realizing the "win-win" situation of economic growth, industrial development and environmental protection.

5.1 China's industrial structure and industrial development

5.1.1 The development of China's industrial structure

Since the reform and opening up in 1978, the government has attached great importance to the issue of industrial structure. During the ensuing 40 years of reform and opening up, the government has promulgated many industrial structure policies to promote industrial restructuring and upgrading. Especially under the increasingly serious contradiction between economic growth and environmental pollution, it is of vital importance to adjust the industrial structure and promote the transformation and upgrading of China's economic structure. Generally speaking, the proportion of the output

58 Industrial structure upgrading

value of China's three industries – primary, secondary, and tertiary – is constantly changing. The structures of these three industries have also undergone substantial changes, and the trend of industrial structure upgrading has been continuously presented. The upgrading of China's industrial structure is largely influenced by the government's industrial structure policies. The direction of industrial development is constantly changing and adjusting. Therefore, along with the development process of China's reform and opening up, the upgrading of industrial structure has its periodic characteristics. We have summarized the three industrial patterns of the national economy and the key development industries in the planning period from reform and opening up to the 13th Five-Year Plan, as shown in Table 5.1 (for more information, see, for example, Shi, 2017).

In order to facilitate the analysis of changes in industrial structure policies, we use the qualitative change point of the three industrial output values as the time node for the evolution of China's industrial structure. The evolution of the industrial structure since China's reform and opening up in 1978 has been divided into three stages.

1   From 1978 to 1984, the three industrial structures of each year showed the structural pattern of "secondary industry, primary industry, tertiary industry". In 1978, the proportion of the three industrial structures was 27.9%, 47.56% and 24.54%, respectively. In 1984, the three industrial structures were further improved to 31.77%, 42.76% and 25.48%, and the proportion of the secondary industry ranked first in the national economy. At this stage, the state continued to put agriculture in an important strategic position, promoting the further development of agriculture and adjusting the service direction and product structure of heavy industry. As a result, the proportion of the primary industry increased and the proportion of the secondary industry declined. In addition, the proportion of tertiary industry increased.

2   From 1985 to 2011, the three industrial structures of each year showed the structural pattern of "secondary industry, tertiary industry, primary industry". In 1985, the proportion of the three industrial structures was 28.12%, 42.55% and 29.33%, respectively. In 2011, the proportion of the three industrial structures was 9.43%, 46.4%, and 44.16%. It can be concluded that China's industrial structure was continuously adjusted and upgraded at this stage. With regard to primary industry, China achieved remarkable results in promoting agricultural modernization, adjusting the agricultural industrial structure and transforming agricultural growth methods. With regard to the secondary industry, China reorganized and transformed industrial enterprises, thereby completely

Table 5.1 China's Industrial Structure and Development (1981–2020)

Period	Three Industrial Patterns	Key Development Directions
1981–1985 (Sixth Five-Year Plan period)	Secondary industry, primary industry, tertiary industry	Adjusting the service direction and product structure of heavy industry, agriculture, energy and transportation and consumer goods industry (light textile products and daily industrial products)
1986–1990 (Seventh Five-Year Plan period)	Secondary industry, tertiary industry, primary industry	Further rational adjustment of the industrial structure and development of tertiary industry, energy, transportation, communications, raw materials industry and consumer goods industry
1991–1995 (Eighth Five-Year Plan period)	Secondary industry, tertiary industry, primary industry	Vigorously adjusting the industrial structure; strengthening the construction of agriculture, basic industries and infrastructure; reorganizing and transforming the processing industry; promoting the rationalization of the industrial structure and gradually moving toward modernization; paying attention to the development of the tertiary industry, agriculture, energy industry, transportation, post and telecommunications, raw materials industry, electronics industry, machinery manufacturing industry, textile industry and construction industry
1996–2000 (Ninth Five-Year Plan period)	Secondary industry, tertiary industry, primary industry	Actively promoting the adjustment of industrial structure, actively developing the tertiary industry, continuing to strengthen infrastructure and basic industries (water, energy, transportation, communications and important raw materials industries) and vigorously revitalizing the pillar industries (mechanics, electronics, petrochemicals, automobiles and construction) and developing the textile industry

(*Continued*)

Table 5.1 Continued

Period	Three Industrial Patterns	Key Development Directions
2001–2005 (10th Five-Year Plan period)	Secondary industry, tertiary industry, primary industry	Promoting industrial structure optimization and upgrading, strengthening the basic position of agriculture, optimizing the industrial structure, actively developing high-tech industries and emerging industries, developing service industries, and accelerating the development of the information industry.
2006–2010 (11th Five-Year Plan period)	Secondary industry, tertiary industry, primary industry	Optimizing the industrial structure; taking the adjustment of the economic structure as the main line; promoting the transformation of economic growth to the synergy of the three industries to achieve optimization and upgrading; developing modern agriculture and promoting the adjustment of agricultural industrial structure; accelerating the development of high-tech industries; and revitalizing the equipment manufacturing industry (technical equipment, automobile industry, shipbuilding industry), energy industry, raw material industry and textile industry
2011–2015 (12th Five-Year Plan period)	Tertiary industry, secondary industry, primary industry	Promoting the development of the service industry as the strategic focus of the optimization and upgrading of the industrial structure, cultivating and developing strategic emerging industries and promoting the adjustment of key industrial structures (equipment manufacturing, shipbuilding, automotive, metallurgy and building materials, petrochemical, textile, packaging, electronic information, construction)
2016–2020 (13th Five-Year Plan period)	In the process of development and change	Optimizing the allocation of elements and promoting the upgrading of industrial structure, the cultural industry becoming a pillar industry of the national economy, promoting agricultural modernization and agricultural industrial restructuring, accelerating the promotion of high-quality and efficient development of the service industry and supporting strategic emerging industries (new generation information technology industry, bio-industry, energy storage and distributed energy, high-end materials, new energy vehicles)

reversing the priority growth of heavy industry. China emphasized the transformation of industry from epitaxial development to connotative development, which has led to a significant increase in resource utilization efficiency, and the vigorous development of high-tech industries and strategic emerging industries. Regarding the tertiary industry, China started the tertiary industry in the period of the Seventh Five-Year Plan and vigorously developed the tertiary industry in the period of the 11th Five-Year Plan. Eventually, China completely reversed the concept of attaching importance to industrial development but neglecting the development of the tertiary industry, causing the proportion of the tertiary industry to rapidly increase.

3   From 2012 to the present, the three industrial structures of each year have a structural pattern of "tertiary industry, secondary industry, primary industry". In 2012, the proportion of the three industrial structures was 9.42%, 45.27% and 45.31%, respectively. We can see that the industrial structure has changed into the pattern of "tertiary industry, secondary industry, primary industry". This stage is characterized by the tertiary industry further rising to prominence, indicating the significant development of China's tertiary industry in the past 40 years. Agriculture in China continues to maintain steady growth, and the gap between urban and rural areas is shrinking. With the development of new industrialization and urbanization, China has gradually established a modern industrial system that has promoted the upgrading of China's industrial structure and improved China's industrial core competitiveness. What's more, the consumption structure of Chinese residents

Table 5.2 GDP and the Three Major Industrial Output Values of China (100 million yuan)

Year	GDP	Primary Industry	Secondary Industry	Tertiary Industry
2008	319515.5	32753.2	149956.6	136805.8
2009	349081.4	34161.8	160171.7	154747.9
2010	413030.3	39362.6	191629.8	182038.0
2011	489300.6	46163.1	227038.8	216098.6
2012	540367.4	50902.3	244643.3	244821.9
2013	595244.4	55329.1	261956.1	277959.3
2014	643974.0	58343.5	277571.8	308058.6
2015	689052.1	60862.1	282040.3	346149.7
2016	743585.5	63672.8	296547.7	383365.0
2017	827121.7	65467.6	334622.6	427031.5

Source: China Statistical Yearbook (various issues)

62 Industrial structure upgrading

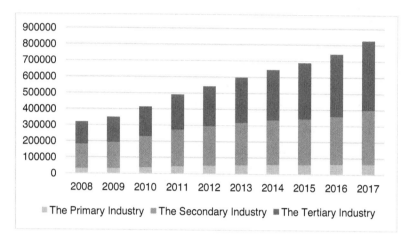

Figure 5.1 China's Three Major Industrial Output Values in 2008–2017

has been further upgraded and the consumption rate has been continuously improved, indicating that people's living standards have further improved (Shi, 2017).

It can be seen that since the reform and opening up China has experienced the evolution of the industrial structure from the three major industrial structures of "secondary industry, primary industry and tertiary industry" to "secondary industry, tertiary industry and primary industry" and then the "tertiary industry, secondary industry and primary industry". In the comprehensive environmental management stage of China, the proportion of the three industries has undergone a qualitative change, and the industrial structure has been upgraded significantly. Table 5.2 and Figure 5.1 show the GDP and the comparison of three major industrial output values of China from 2008 to 2017.

5.1.2 Industrial structure upgrading in different regions of China

Over the years, China's industrial restructuring has achieved significant results, as shown in Table 5.3. However, differences remain in the speed and trend of industrial structure upgrading in the eastern, central and western regions of China. The upgrading trend of industrial structure in the eastern region is more obvious than that in the central and western regions.

It can be seen that the three major industrial trends in China's eastern, central and western regions from 2008 to 2017 are generally consistent with the general nationwide trend. All regions show that the proportion of the primary industry in the national economy has gradually declined, the

Table 5.3 Three Industrial Output Value Structures in the Eastern, Central and Western Regions of China (%)

Year	Nationwide Primary Industry	Nationwide Secondary Industry	Nationwide Tertiary Industry	Eastern Region Primary Industry	Eastern Region Secondary Industry	Eastern Region Tertiary Industry	Central Region Primary Industry	Central Region Secondary Industry	Central Region Tertiary Industry	Western Region Primary Industry	Western Region Secondary Industry	Western Region Tertiary Industry
2008	10.34	46.76	42.91	7.04	51.95	41.01	14.42	50.85	34.73	15.56	48.10	36.34
2009	9.88	45.67	44.45	6.74	49.53	43.72	13.58	49.93	36.49	13.73	47.46	38.81
2010	9.62	46.17	44.20	6.49	49.72	43.79	12.91	52.16	34.93	13.15	49.99	36.87
2011	9.53	46.14	44.32	5.93	49.48	44.58	12.02	54.22	33.76	11.32	52.36	36.32
2012	9.53	44.97	45.50	5.89	48.41	45.70	11.94	53.50	34.57	11.00	52.17	36.83
2013	9.41	43.67	46.92	5.81	47.50	46.68	11.71	52.80	35.49	10.79	51.16	38.05
2014	9.17	42.72	48.11	5.49	45.93	48.58	11.33	50.94	37.74	10.36	49.06	40.58
2015	8.31	43.69	42.09	5.83	43.44	50.73	10.84	43.48	40.69	11.97	44.64	43.39
2016	8.24	41.52	49.70	5.57	42.10	52.56	11.46	38.92	46.77	11.87	42.95	45.18
2017	7.33	42.01	50.30	4.89	41.48	52.99	9.58	43.89	45.53	11.39	41.19	47.42

Source: China Statistical Yearbook (various issues)

proportion of the secondary industry in the national economy has fluctuated and the proportion of the tertiary industry in the national economy has gradually increased. The main reason for this trend is that China promotes agricultural modernization and develops high-tech, strategic emerging industries and high value–added industries. At the same time, China vigorously develops the tertiary industry and attaches great importance to the development of the service industry. From 2008 to 2017, China's three industrial structure types of "secondary industry, tertiary industry, primary industry" were transformed into "tertiary industry, secondary industry, primary industry" industrial structure types. However, it is worth noting that the industrial structure types and the timing of qualitative change of the proportion of the three industries in the eastern, central and western regions of China are not consistent with the general trend for the whole country. In the eastern region, the proportion of the three industries had undergone a qualitative change by 2014. The industrial structure changed from "secondary industry, tertiary industry, primary industry" to "tertiary industry, secondary industry, primary industry". This change occurred in the central and western regions in 2016. It can be seen that in the process of industrial structure transformation and upgrading in China, the eastern region has the most outstanding performance and has contributed the most to China's economic restructuring.

5.2 Environmental regulation and industrial development issues

At present, the Chinese economy has entered a "new normal". On the one hand, China must strengthen environmental regulations to improve environmental quality, and on the other hand, it should promote the transformation and upgrading of industrial structure. It is an important issue that needs to be solved soon in order to stimulate the potential growth of the economy through the benign interaction of environmental and industrial structure transformation and upgrading. The problems of environmental regulation and industrial structure upgrading in China are as follows.

5.2.1 The imperfect market-based environmental regulation

In 2002, China joined the World Trade Organization (WTO). The degree of economic openness has further expanded and the marketization process has accelerated compared with the past. Environmental problems in China have gradually evolved from single, specific issues to more complex and comprehensive types of pollution. Environmental pollution is gradually transmitted and spread to China through world economic channels such

Industrial structure upgrading 65

as international trade and foreign direct investment due to the increasingly open market. Market-based environmental regulation in China has indeed been vigorously developed, but there are still many shortcomings and problems in solving the contradiction between China's rapid economic growth and environmental problems under the current open economic structure, which restricts China's industrial development:

1 In July 2016, the Notice on Expanding Reform of Resource Taxes implemented the comprehensive ad valorem collection of China's resource tax. With this notice, a resource tax on products in China was combined with the price, indicating that more attention has been paid to the use of price mechanism to govern China's resource and environment problems. However, at present, the resource price system in China is not perfect, and resource price reform is still in progress, which will make the resource tax, a green tax, play a very limited role in market-oriented environmental regulation (Shi, 2017).
2 Pollution rights trading, a market-based environmental regulation tool, has faced many problems in the process of pilot implementation in China. The policies and mechanisms need to be adjusted and innovated. As early as 1999, the National Environmental Protection Agency and the Environmental Defense Fund jointly launched a pilot project on the use of market mechanisms to control sulfur dioxide emissions in Benxi City, Liaoning Province, and Nantong, Jiangsu Province. In September 2001, a sulfur dioxide emission trading mechanism funded by the Asian Development Bank launched pilot work in Taiyuan, Shanxi Province. In 2007, 11 provinces and cities, including Jiangsu Province and Zhejiang Province, launched pilot projects on emissions trading. However, some problems have gradually emerged in these pilot provinces of China, including inactive emission trading, inconsistent types and scope of environmental pollution applicable to emission trading policies, unclear boundary conditions for determining the price of emission trading, unclear conditions for carrying out emission trading and inconsistent transaction prices of initial pollution rights trading due to the different economic bases of the provinces. In addition, there are differences in environmental quality and capacity among provinces, which affect the implementation of the system.
3 The overall environmental problems in China are still grim and the ecological environment pollution has not been effectively curbed. At present, China's environmental protection efforts are gradually increasing, and the demand for funds is large. It seems simplistic and weak to solve the problem of raising environmental protection funds by order-control environmental regulation and relying on the

66 *Industrial structure upgrading*

government's investment in environmental governance. In fact, the current total amount of investment and financing for environmental protection in China is insufficient and inefficient and the important role of market in raising environmental protection funds has not been brought into full play. Although the Third Plenary Session of the 18th CPC Central Committee put forward the idea of "establishing a market-oriented mechanism for absorbing social capital to invest in ecological environmental protection", the scale and proportion of social capital investment are not high at present. The investment and financing policy as well as development mode of environmental protection need to be innovated. At the same time, the enthusiasm of social capital to invest in ecological environment protection should be further improved.

4   There are regional differences in the economic development of the eastern, central and western regions of China. Compared with the eastern region, the economic development level in the central region is not high and the economy in the western region is underdeveloped. In this economic development pattern, the central and western regions are both facing severe resource and environmental problems. However, the level of market-oriented environmental regulation in the central and western regions of China is not high.

5.2.2 Imperfect information disclosure–public participation environmental regulation

The construction of information disclosure–public participation environmental regulation in China started relatively late, which is affected by many factors, such as the economy, law, policy, system, population quality, citizen consciousness and so on. Its effect on industrial structure upgrading is unsteady. Information disclosure–public participation type environmental regulation is an informal environmental regulation. Its regulatory function is influenced by many subjective factors, and thus the effect will be unstable. As early as 1994, China began to carry out environmental labeling work and information disclosure-based environmental regulation began to be implemented. The Environmental Impact Assessment Law in 2002 formally established public participation environmental regulation in China. However, compared with the construction of command-control and market-based environmental regulation, it started late. China is a developing country and the environmental labeling and environmental certification work in China lags behind that of developed countries in the West. For a long time, the media and the public did not pay much attention to environmental issues. However, with the increasingly frequent occurrence of fog and haze in China environmental protection issues gradually became the focus of media and public attention. The population of different regions in China is different in educational levels and personal qualities, which leads to the different awareness and consciousness of environmental protection. Therefore, the attitudes, reactions and behaviors of the residents towards environmental protection will be different in different periods and different stages of development. As a result, China needs to further improve the information disclosure and public participation policies and regulations related to environmental regulation. The government of China should improve the participation mechanism and establish relevant cooperation measures to promote the positive and effective impact of information disclosure–public participation environmental regulation in China.

5.2.3 Insufficient labor productivity in China's industries

Although the industrial structure upgrading in China has changed greatly in the total output value of the three industries and the proportion among the three industries has changed, labor productivity still needs to be further improved. China's industrial structure is constantly adjusting and upgrading, but the relative labor productivity of various industries has not increased significantly. The reason is related to the long-term adoption of the extension of industrial structure adjustment methods in China. China mainly emphasizes the use of the external power of industry and resources to adjust the industrial structure and pays attention to the growth of industrial output value and scale. But it ignores the endogenous power of industrial restructuring and fails to effectively integrate the upgrading of industrial structure with the improvement of the scientific and technological level of labor force and the allocation of factor markets in this industry, which makes the relative labor productivity of various industries not effectively improved in the process of China's industrial structure upgrading. The relative labor productivity of China's primary industry is relatively low, indicating that the output value created by the primary industry is much lower than the labor consumed by it. There is still much room for improvement in the labor productivity of China's primary industry. On the basis of the existing labor force, the primary industry should create higher output values. On the other hand, a large quantity of labor in China has flowed out of the primary industry and gradually flowed into the secondary and tertiary industries. The new allocation of labor has increased the total output of the society, and made the three major industrial structures adjust and upgrade gradually. Since 2002, a large number of laborers in China have flowed to the secondary and tertiary industries. However, the wages of workers in China have been low for a long time. The long-term low wages and low labor costs have hindered technological progress and industrial structure upgrading. It also has weakened the effect of industrial structure upgrading. Therefore, the relative labor productivity of China's secondary and tertiary industries has not increased significantly with the upgrading of industrial structure.

5.2.4 Sluggish upgrading in the central and western regions

The overall industrial structure in China has an obvious trend of upgrading, and the industrial structure development pattern has undergone qualitative changes, becoming the structural type of "tertiary industry, secondary industry, primary industry". But the industrial structure types and the timing of qualitative changes of the proportion of the three industries in the eastern, central and western regions are inconsistent with the general trend of the whole country. In the eastern region, the proportion of the three industries demonstrated a qualitative change in 2014, with its industrial structure shifting from "secondary industry, tertiary industry, primary industry" to "tertiary industry, secondary industry, and primary industry". The same change occurred in the central and western regions in 2016. It can be seen that in the process of industrial structure transformation and upgrading in China, the performance of the eastern region is the most prominent, and it has contributed the most to China's economic restructuring. In recent years, the eastern region of China has accelerated its economic restructuring and shifted many industries to the central and western regions. There are obvious regional differences in R&D agglomeration, knowledge spillover, market potential and wage level across the eastern, central and western regions of China. In addition, the industries that have been transferred from the eastern region to the central and western regions are mostly those with low technology content, high pollution and high energy consumption. Therefore, the industrial transfer in the eastern region of China only promotes the optimization and upgrading of its own regional industrial structure, and does not effectively promote the upgrading of industrial structure in the central and western regions. On the contrary, it aggravates the burden of ecological environment in the central and western regions.

5.2.5 The insufficient quality and efficiency of industrial structure upgrading

China has a problem of overcapacity, and the industrial structure upgrade still adopts the factor-driven approach. In the second half of 2002, due to long-term expansion investment, some industries, such as steel and cement, experienced overcapacity during the 12th Five-Year Plan period. Resource prices have long been distorted in China, and the ad valorem taxation

Industrial structure upgrading 69

reform of the resource tax has been in place since 2010. Resource prices in China did not reflect the real exhaustion value of resources. Therefore, industries with excess capacity consumed a lot of resources in China for a long time. This led to waste of resources and even resource shortages. From 2000 to 2011, the proportion of losses caused by resource depletion and environmental damage in China increased from 5.3% to 8.4% (Liu and Li, 2018). Although the proportion of the output value of the three industries in China shows the industrial structure of the "tertiary industry, secondary industry, primary industry", the development speed and employment absorption capacity of the tertiary industry (service industry) in China is still not high (Liu and Xu, 2017). The problem of overcapacity and resource consumption is still severe. In addition, labor productivity and the ability to absorb employment have not been greatly improved. Thus, the quality and efficiency of industrial structure upgrading need to be further improved. Up to the end of the 12th Five-Year Plan period, the industrial structure upgrading in China still adopted a factor-driven approach, which lacked efficiency and innovation. Problems such as the distortion of resource valuation in the process of industrial structure upgrading are due to the government's support and guidance of some industries. In addition, the population size and the pattern of economic growth in China have led to the accumulation of a large number of labor- and capital-intensive industries and underdevelopment of technology-intensive industries. At present, many industries still remain at the low end of the industrial chain and value chain. The added value of the product is not high enough, which is not conducive to the upgrading of the industrial structure (Shi, 2017).

5.3 Policy recommendations

The implementation of different environmental regulatory measures is beneficial to the optimization and upgrading of China's industrial structure. After the implementation of environmental regulations, enterprises and individuals will increase their awareness of environmental protection and reduce pollution emissions. The consumption and production structure will develop into a green form, driving the industrial structure to move toward rationalization and heightening. It also can reduce the negative external influence of environmental pollution and give the market an important role in promoting sustainability. In addition, it can stimulate enterprises into innovating technology, which will promote the development of high-tech industries to accelerate the upgrading of industrial structure. At the same time, it will make economic development break through the constraints of the environment and resources to realize harmonious development (Wang, 2018). Overall, the industrial structure in China is constantly being optimized and upgraded, but the level of economic development is very different due to the uneven development of regions. In order to achieve the common development of the economy and the environment, the following policy recommendations in light of China's actual situation are put forward.

5.3.1 Policy recommendations at the micro level

Enterprises are the basic unit of the industry. Each industry is composed of a large number of enterprises that interact with one another. The development trend of an industry is inseparable from the development trend of the various enterprises within the industry. The development of the enterprise will directly affect the development of the industry and the development pattern of each industry will drive the change of the overall industrial structure. It can be seen that the transformation and upgrading of enterprises directly affects the transformation and upgrading of the industry. In other words, the transformation and upgrading of the industry is closely related to the industrial structure. Therefore, the development of the enterprise plays a micro-basic role in industrial structure upgrading (Shi, 2017). In order to enable enterprises to develop better and to transform and upgrade smoothly under environmental regulations to promote the upgrading of industrial structure, specific policy recommendations based on the micro level (enterprise level) are put forward from three aspects of technological innovation, industrial added value and development strategy, as well as effective use of financial products and tools.

5.3.1.1 Attaching great importance to technological innovation

Enterprises should actively innovate in technology and improve the level of technological innovation. They are supposed to change from "end-of-pipe treatment" to "containment from the source". Under the situation of increasingly stringent environmental regulation policies, enterprises should adopt positive and sustainable countermeasures, and strengthen technological innovation to promote enterprise transformation and upgrading. Instead of relying on "end-of-pipe treatment" to passively respond to environmental regulations, they should focus on "containment from the source". First, technological innovation should be carried out in the production of products to improve the utilization efficiency of production raw materials and to improve the manufacturing process. The machinery and equipment should also be updated and upgraded. In addition, enterprises can independently develop new products, new processes or new technologies and adopt advanced production equipment. They can improve resource utilization efficiency through effective integration and rational allocation of resources to reduce enterprise costs. The new products, new processes and new technologies introduced by enterprises should take into account the dual attributes of commercial value and environmental value. They should not only obtain economic benefits, but also protect the ecological environment and conserve resources. Enterprises should advance with the times. Enterprises need to improve their ability to implement scientific and technological advancements. They should keep abreast of the latest developments of relevant scientific research technologies or achievements in their fields and invest funds to purchase or legally acquire scientific research achievements created by others. On this basis, the advanced and high-quality scientific research achievements should be effectively transformed and utilized to enhance the technological progress of enterprises. In addition, if enterprises want to vigorously improve the level of technological innovation, a high-quality and efficient talent team and a good environment and conditions for technological innovation are indispensable. Therefore, enterprises should actively recruit high-quality talent. What's more, working conditions, hardware and software should also foster technological innovation. Last but not least, enterprises should establish a corporate ideology and cultural atmosphere that emphasizes and pursues technological innovation.

5.3.1.2 Improving the added value of products effectively

Increasing the added value of products mainly means increasing the value created by intellectual labor in the production process and circulation. The high added value of the product will enable enterprises to obtain higher economic benefits. To increase the added value of products, enterprises should consider not only the function, quality and technical content of the products, but also whether the products satisfy the subjective needs of customers. First, enterprises must increase the high-tech composition and improve the technical content. Increasing investment in product research and development can help to increase the added value of the product in the production process and enhance the function of the product. In addition, it can also guarantee the quality of the product. Second, while diversifying the production of products, enterprises should also pursue the characteristics of individualized appeals and explore the characteristics of products. They should combine the performance, design and packaging of the products with market segmentation to increase the added value of the product in the circulation, thus forming a competitive advantage in the market. In addition, the cultural characteristic of the product is also a part of the added value of the product. China is a country with profound cultural history, and each province has its own unique and colorful local culture. With the improvement of living standards, people pay more attention to the cultural connotation of products in addition to the performance and quality of products. Therefore, exploring the cultural characteristics of products helps to improve the level and taste of products, which is also a part of improving the added value of products. Finally, enterprises should not only sell products but also satisfy their customers. At the same time, they should win the loyalty of customers in the face of fierce market competition. This helps to increase the added value of the product in the sales process. What's more, enterprises should also upgrade their development strategies and transform their development strategies that are not suitable for environmental protection and ecological civilization construction. In the process of formulating the development strategy, it is necessary to integrate the economic concept of sustainable development so that enterprises can take into account the responsibility of environmental protection while improving economic efficiency. Finally, the company will develop into a green enterprise with good economic benefits, strong market competitiveness and energy conservation, as well as environmental protection.

5.3.1.3 Using financial instruments to deal with environmental regulatory risks

With the increasingly stringent environmental regulation, projects such as corporate governance environment, technological innovation and equipment upgrading will increase expenditures and require funds. The innovative compensation effect generated by the technological innovation of enterprises due to environmental regulation will take some time to be reflected. Therefore, in the short term, the company will increase production costs because of the increase of various project expenses, which will have a temporary impact on the company's profit. In this case, companies effectively use financial products or financial instruments to deal with the various risks that environmental regulations bring to the production and operation of enterprises. For example, enterprises should actively participate in pollution rights trading. They can also make comprehensive assessments based on their own characteristics and use debt financing methods reasonably. In addition, enterprises can rationally use relevant financial products, financial instruments or financial services to solve problems such as project investment and financing, project operation and risk management in the process of green transformation and upgrading.

5.3.2 Policy recommendations at the meso level

Industrial development and industrial policies have a direct impact on the upgrading of industrial structure. The market mechanism will play an important role in the development of innovative industries and elimination of backward industries, which will promote industrial transformation and upgrading and result in competitive and well-developed industries that can successfully compete in the market. The development of industry is the basis for the upgrading of industrial structure. The industrial policy reflects the government's intervention and guidance on industrial development and industrial restructuring. It plays a dual role in upgrading industrial structure. On the one hand, it supports industries with weak development capabilities and weak competitiveness but that are in line with the concept of sustainable development and that in the long run will contribute to the upgrading of industrial structure. On the other hand, the government sometimes invests in enterprises based on immediate economic interests without considering the long-term development interests. Such short-sighted behavior will hinder the upgrading of the industrial structure. Therefore, industrial policy is a "double-edged sword" and needs to be applied reasonably and effectively. The formulation and implementation of industrial policies need to be combined with effective markets and government promises to promote industrial structure upgrading. The policy recommendations based on the meso level are proposed on the two aspects of industrial development and industrial policy.

5.3.2.1 Focusing on improving the total factor productivity of the industry

The total factor productivity of the industry mainly comes from technological progress, organizational innovation, production innovation and specialization. Its essence is to improve the technological progress of the industry. Only by improving the total factor productivity of industry can the mode of industrial development be transformed from the investment-driven type to the efficiency-driven type and from the extensive-growth type to the intensive-growth type. Then it will promote the transformation of industrial structure upgrading mode from extension to deepening.

To improve the total factor productivity of the industry, the development mode of the industry should be changed from relying on natural resources, labor and capital factor inputs to relying more on industrial technology innovation and high-quality human resources. What's more, the efficiency and competitiveness of the industry should be emphasized. Innovation includes two aspects: technological innovation and institutional innovation. The industrial total factor productivity can reflect the level of innovation and development of the industry. Therefore, it is necessary to promote the upgrading of industrial structure by increasing the total factor productivity of the industry.

An industry's total factor productivity can be increased by improving the efficiency of resource allocation. But how to effectively improve the efficiency of resource allocation in the industry? On the one hand, the industry should improve the efficiency of resource allocation by re-integrating production factors. Re-integration of production factors can break some barriers through urbanization and innovation of institutional mechanisms so that production factors can flow freely from inefficient sectors to efficient sectors. On the other hand, China should accelerate the upgrading of the industrial structure of the manufacturing and service industries to improve the efficiency of resource allocation within the industry. Under the strategic background of "Made in China 2025" plan, "Internet plus" and other national action plans, the country should seize the opportunity to transform and upgrade the traditional manufacturing industry and re-integrate enterprises within the industry. China should cultivate strategic emerging industries and high-tech industries and vigorously develop modern service industries. In addition, market mechanisms should have a key role in efficient resource allocation. Deepening reform, promoting institutional and institutional innovation, improving industrial competition and exit mechanisms, reducing ineffective interventions in industrial development and achieving the survival of the fittest within the industry are all important ways to improve industrial competitiveness and overall efficiency.

Total factor productivity can be increased through factor agglomeration. Factor agglomeration includes agglomeration of material capital elements, agglomeration of human capital elements, agglomeration of labor factors and agglomeration of innovative elements. These factor agglomerations will gradually form economies of scale and brand effects that contribute to the development of the industry. It is conducive to organizational innovation and production innovation. At the same time, it helps to save resources and improve the efficiency of resource utilization, ultimately promoting the improvement of industrial total factor productivity.

5.3.2.2 Shifting the industry to the high-end link of the value chain

China has entered a new mode of economic development. China has gradually changed from the rapid growth of scale and speed to the intensive growth of quality and efficiency. Its economic development relies more on economic restructuring and innovation-driven development. It is constantly taking the extension of the industrial chain and upgrading the industrial value chain as the endogenous driving force of economic development. Extending the industrial chain and upgrading the industrial value chain can effectively expand product supply and enhance the quality and efficiency of enterprises. It will also enhance regional industrial competitiveness, strengthen the shortcomings of the industrial chain and expand new

Industrial structure upgrading 75

markets. In the era of "Internet plus", it helps to fully explore the market potential and transform traditional industries. Furthermore, it is conducive to cultivate more emerging industries and eliminate backward production capacity to promote the construction of a new modern industrial system and ultimately promote the upgrading of industrial structure.

The extension of the industrial chain must adhere to the direction of green development. It should promote the development of green industry and the development of green products. So, China should vigorously develop energy-saving, environmentally friendly industries as well as clean production projects to eliminate polluting projects.

China should complement the industrial chain through stocks. On the one hand, we could rely on the park economy, enterprise interaction and industrial clusters to enable the industrial chain to be coupled to each other so that they complement the industrial chain. On the other hand, it is also necessary to extend the industrial chain through industrial complementarity, resource location advantages and high-end manufacturing. The complementarity of the industrial chain among large enterprises and small and medium-sized enterprises should be emphasized. In addition, the industrial value chain should be upgraded by enhancing industrial advantages and improving the technological content and standards of the industry.

China should integrate the actual conditions and advantages of each place to do a good job in industrial development and overall planning. For example, it could upgrade the industrial value chain in some key industry development areas and promote the transfer of industries to the high-end links of the industrial value chain.

China must provide necessary safeguards for the extension and the upgrading of the industrial value chain. For example, it can strengthen the organizational leadership, enhance overall planning and strongly support enterprise projects in the industry chain. Or it can optimize the environment of industrial development with market orientation and expand the external opening of the economy to protect the external environment of the industrial value chain. It is also necessary to increase fiscal and financial support to ensure financial support for the upgrading of the industrial value chain. In addition, it is also of great importance to improve the talent cultivation and introduction mechanism and to optimize the environment for talent growth and development so as to guarantee the supply of talents in the industrial value chain.

5.3.2.3 Transforming comparative advantages into competitive advantages

Industrial development should refer to the comparative advantages of the region where the industry is located and transform the comparative advantage into a competitive advantage. The upgrading of industrial structure should be promoted through marketing, innovation and upgrading of factor endowments.

The upgrading of industrial structure needs to refer to comparative advantages, but it should not fall into the trap of "comparative advantage" where it will not make progress. The long-term overreliance on comparative advantage in industrial development may lead to the suppression of technological innovation, which results in the risk of slow effect, long time, high investment and high cost of technological innovation. Local governments and companies tend to focus on the development of labor-intensive industries for a long period of time, while paying less attention to the development of technology-intensive industries. Labor-intensive industries have the characteristics of consuming a large number of production factors such as labor, land, capital, etc., which will form an extrusion effect on the factors of industrial technology upgrading and innovation, and weaken the ability of the industry to withstand technological risks and market risks in the development process. What's more, it is also not conducive to the extension of the industrial chain and the upgrading of the value chain. In addition, in the context of economic openness, if the industry is in the low-end link of the industrial value chain relying on comparative advantage for a long time, its industrial profits may be squeezed and weakened in the transnational economic cooperation so that the industrial development may ignore technological innovation and R&D links for a long time, which will lock the industry in the low-end of the global value chain.

China should accelerate the upgrading of factor endowment structure and transform the comparative advantage of industrial development into a competitive advantage. On the one hand, China should improve the formation mechanism of factor market and factor price as well as the efficiency of factor allocation. It is necessary to reform and improve the price formation mechanism of production factors and fully utilize the regulatory role of the market to reflect the scarcity of resources and the relationship between market supply and demand. The cost accounting system for production factors should be improved such that resource prices reflect the true cost of resources and the environment, especially with regard to non-renewable resources. It is of vital importance for improving resource utilization efficiency, energy conservation and emission reduction, as well as protecting the ecological environment. In addition, market mechanisms should be used to correct price distortions in production factors and improve the quality of capital and labor factors. On the other hand, it is necessary to be based on the global value chain and promote the transformation and upgrading of the factor endowment structure. Under the global value chain division of labor system, the price of various elements, the proportion of factors and the way in which the elements are used will change, which will change the structure of factor endowments. The factor endowment structure will directly affect the industrial structure and trade structure. Therefore, it is important to upgrade the factor endowment structure and improve the competitive advantage of industrial development. In this way, industrial development will be promoted into the high-end links of the global value chain.

5.3.2.4 Paying attention to the development of the cultural industry

With the improvement of China's economic and social development, the development of cultural industry has become a new economic growth point. Vigorous development of the cultural industry has become an important component in the process of industrial restructuring in China. In fact, the development of cultural industry can promote the upgrading of industrial structure indirectly. Cultural industry policy has become an important policy for China's industrial development. Unfortunately, the economic growth and development of China has followed the old road of "pollution first, then treatment" of developed countries for a long time. The local economic growth of many provinces and cities in China mostly relies on local mineral resources or other types of characteristic natural resources. However, many of these natural resources are consumptive. When the resources of some cities are used to a certain extent or even exhausted, the economic development of the city will gradually decline. There will gradually be a lack of competitiveness and development stamina in these cities. This is becoming more evident in the economic development of some resource-based cities. As a result, these cities are pursuing transformation and upgrading. It is undeniable that the resource-driven economic growth mode of the past is no longer sustainable. China is a country rich in history and culture, with 5000 years of civilization. Each province or city has its own local characteristics and culture. The 18th National Congress of the Communist Party of China explicitly proposed the vigorous development of cultural industries. Some local governments have also introduced plans and specific measures for the development of cultural industries. Cultural industry has the dual attributes of ideology and commodity. It can not only bring economic benefits to the overall national and local economic development, but it also brings social benefits. In addition, the development of the cultural industry is conducive to improving the cultural literacy of citizens and cultivating their sentiments. Improving the quality of citizens while developing the economy can provide intangible help for environmental protection and industrial structure upgrading.

The development of cultural industries is inseparable from the cultivation and development of cultural enterprises. The scale, quantity and quality of cultural enterprises are directly related to the development prospects of cultural industries. Therefore, a number of high-quality cultural enterprises should be cultivated in all parts of China and the local characteristic culture should be fully integrated to create a local cultural characteristic brand effect. At the same time, it is also possible to use the relevant departments of local governments to lead and cooperate with various cultural enterprises to establish local cultural enterprise development associations, which helps to build an effective platform for information resource sharing and policy communication for local cultural industry development and to promote the development of cultural enterprises.

It is necessary to build a complete cultural industry chain. The development of the cultural industry is closely related to various industries such as information, manufacturing and logistics. Therefore, the development of the cultural industry must be integrated with other industries. For example, cultural creative products or clothes with local cultural characteristics requires the cooperation of the manufacturing industry, and the sale of cultural products requires the cooperation of the logistics industry. The cultural industry can also serve as the engine for the development of local industries, driving the development of local industries in the upper, middle and lower reaches.

The central and local governments need to formulate relevant policies and supporting measures to support the development of the cultural industry such as supporting cultural industry construction through financial funds and guiding social capital participation, cultivating professional talents related to cultural industry development and carrying out cultural industry quality courses in universities, encouraging cultural industry's characteristic innovation and cultural product design, and promulgating relevant laws and regulations to protect intellectual property rights, product patents, trademarks and brands of the cultural industry.

5.3.2.5 Preventing the hollowing out of the industry

According to the evolution law of industrial structure upgrading, the proportion of the three industries of the national economy will change, and the tertiary industry (service industry) will gradually occupy an important position in the national economy, and eventually the proportion of the tertiary industry will account for more than 50% (this was achieved in 2017). First, we have to admit the fact that the development of the service industry will indeed promote the upgrading of the industrial structure. However, while the service industry is developing vigorously, we should not neglect the development of industry. After all, the steady development of industry is the foundation of the economic development of the country. The real industries provide raw materials and other supplies for the economic development of a country, and provide consumers with goods such as clothing, food, shelter and daily use. For a country with a large population like China, if only the service industry is developed but the development of agriculture and industry is neglected, then there will be a hollowing out of industrial development, which means that the virtual industries such as service industry lack the support and supply of agriculture and industry. Once this happens, it is extremely unfavorable for China's economic development. Therefore, while upgrading the industrial structure, we should also coordinate the development of the primary and secondary industries so that the three industries can develop harmoniously and finally optimize the industrial structure. Although some European and Asian countries, such as Japan and South Korea, have experienced the benefits of "tertiarization" and have enjoyed the dividend of industrial structure upgrade in recent years, there are some disadvantages of "tertiarization". There are not only economic reasons, but also social and political reasons for these problems. Therefore, "tertiarization" cannot be completely negated due to the economic development problems in these countries. But at least there are good reasons to believe that it is not objective enough. So how can China avoid the hollowing out of the industry while it is serving the economy?

The basic status of China's agriculture cannot be shaken. It is necessary to ensure the area of cultivated land and food security. It is unwise to erode the area of cultivated land in order to develop real estate and other industries. Agricultural labor productivity should be improved through various favorable measures and effectively promote the rapid development of agricultural production in the direction of science and technology as well as intensification.

It is of great importance to reduce the pollution and destruction of the industrial environment through innovation, technological improvement and energy substitution in the process of industrial development and improve the coordination between industrial development and resource ecological environment. The quality of industrial modernization should also be improved to continuously improve the industrial production capacity.

The service industry should continue to be vigorously developed. The service industry has the characteristics and advantages that agriculture and industry cannot replace in reducing social transaction costs and employment absorption capacity. The rapid development of the tertiary industry of a country helps to improve social efficiency. The development of the primary and secondary industries can be promoted through the leadership and creative design of the cultural industry in the process of developing the tertiary industry, which is the significance of building the cultural industry into a local pillar industry in some places. In fact, it is a very favorable measure to prevent the hollowing out of the industry during the upgrading of industrial structure.

5.3.2.6 Eliminating excess and backward capacity effectively

At present, China has done a lot of work in improving the ecological environment and has made some progress. However, the deterioration of China's ecological environment has not been contained, and the level of ecological civilization construction still lags behind the level of economic and social development. Therefore, it is necessary to improve the incentive and restraint mechanism for industrial development and resolutely eliminate backward production capacity to eliminate the adverse effects of backward production capacity on industrial structure upgrading and the ecological environment.

China should scientifically evaluate the production capacity of various industries and carry out various effective ways to resolve excess capacity. The backward production capacity should be resolutely eliminated. The reason is that excess capacity will weaken the competitiveness of the industry so as to affect the development of the industry. The backward production capacity will hinder the adjustment and optimization of the industrial structure.

China should supervise and check the resolution of excess capacity and the elimination of backward production capacity in strict accordance with the standards to ensure that the production capacity is really eliminated.

Relevant resettlement and guarantee work should be done in the process of resolving excess capacity and eliminating backward production capacity. As for the employment problems arising from capacity elimination, the central subsidy funds and related supporting funds should be used to do staff training and corresponding resettlement. In addition, it is necessary to properly handle employment problems arising from the elimination of production capacity through institutional innovation, construction of employment platforms, encouragement of entrepreneurship and expansion of employment channels. It also is important to combine the work of de-capacity with the optimization of industrial layout and the promotion of industrial transformation and upgrading and to provide financial and fiscal policy support for the specific work related to elimination of excess capacity and backward production capacity.

China should strengthen the performance appraisal of de-capacity work and form an effective incentive, supervision and restraint mechanism. Local governments and enterprises that have outstanding performance in resolving excess capacity and eliminating backward production capacity should be commended; localities and enterprises that are not working well should be severely supervised; violations of laws and regulations in the work of de-capacity should be severely punished.

5.3.2.7 Improving the labor productivity level of the industry rapidly

Improving the labor productivity level of the industry is the key to transforming the economic growth mode and crossing the middle-income trap in China. It plays an important role in improving industrial competitiveness and promoting industrial structure upgrading. At present, the labor productivity growth of the industry is slow and the growth rate is decreasing in the process of industrial structure adjustment and upgrading in China, which is mainly caused by the unreasonable labor allocation structure among industries and the reduction of labor productivity of the three industries.

China should optimize the labor allocation structure among industries and accelerate the improvement of the labor productivity of the industry. Market mechanisms should be used to eliminate labor market distortions and improve the efficiency of labor resource allocation. China has not formed an effective labor market in the process of economic restructuring due to the cumulative effect of long-term restrictions on household registration system, resulting in a low efficiency in resource allocation in the labor market. As for the tertiary industry, the tertiary industry has strong employment absorption capacity and high economic efficiency in theory. However, in the actual situation in China, the employment absorptive capacity of the tertiary industry is far from enough. While employment and output increase, the tertiary industry has not significantly improved the overall economic efficiency of the industry. It can be seen that the resource allocation efficiency of the three industrial labor markets in China is not high enough. Therefore, it is necessary to eliminate the distortion of the labor market to improve the labor market. In addition, it is of great importance to promote the free flow of labor to form a benign interaction and effective allocation of labor for the development of the primary industry, secondary industry and tertiary industry. China should improve the efficiency of labor factor allocation through the regulation of market supply and demand mechanisms to link the labor supply with the labor demand of industrial development effectively. Second, China should effectively promote the overall level of labor productivity in the industry by improving the level of labor productivity in various industries. Third, the level of science and technology of the labor force should be developed through education and training to improve the labor productivity of the industry. Fourth, improving labor organization, production management and human resource management will help to raise the level of labor productivity in the industry (Shi, 2017).

5.3.3 Policy recommendations based on the macro level

In the process of ecological civilization construction in China, the environmental regulation system is still not perfect, and it still needs vigorous development and construction. What's more, there are many problems in the upgrading of industrial structure. Therefore, governments at all levels and relevant departments are required to formulate effective macroeconomic policies to promote the development and improvement of environmental regulations and to overcome obstacles in the process of upgrading industrial structure. Thus, various problems existing in upgrading of industrial structure can be effectively solved so that environmental regulation will play an active and effective role in promoting the upgrading of industrial structure. In this way, the win-win situation of economic growth and environmental protection in China will be realized finally.

5.3.3.1 Policy recommendations on finance

The economic functions of local governments should be clarified. It is necessary to standardize the fiscal expenditure behavior of local governments and optimize the fiscal expenditure structure of local governments. What's more, the negative intervention of local governments on industrial restructuring and industrial development should be weakened. It is necessary to clarify the role and function of the government and the market as well as the central government and the local government in the upgrading of industrial structure. China should also clarify the interests and income division between the central and local governments. Specifically, we should standardize tax preferential policies and incorporate eco-environmental indicators into the official promotion assessment system to curb bad competition among governments and avoid the act of seeking local economic growth at the expense of the environment. In addition, the contradiction between economic growth and environmental issues in the western region of China is more prominent and the level of economic development in the western region is relatively low. As a result, it is necessary to increase the transfer payments of the central government in environmental governance so that it will provide effective support in environmental governance.

Effective financial support should be provided for enterprise technology innovation, energy-saving enterprises and high-tech industry development. The central government should make overall arrangements to increase the proportion of scientific research expenditures in fiscal expenditures and provide adequate financial support for technological innovation. It should also encourage local governments to invest in technological innovation and provide complementary measures. On the other hand, local governments should encourage technological innovation through tax reductions, subsidies and other related preferential policies. Energy-saving industries, environmentally-friendly industries and high-tech industries should be vigorously supported.

5.3.3.2 Policy recommendations on education, investment and urbanization

The central government should increase the proportion of education expenditure in fiscal expenditures. It is necessary to increase investment in education in various regions, especially in the underdeveloped provinces of central and western China. It is also important to improve the efficiency of the use of education funds and design effective mechanisms to enable the underdeveloped western regions to share high-quality educational resources in the eastern region. What's more, human capital should be provided for the upgrading of industrial structure.

Local governments should optimize investment scale of fixed assets and investment structure, and rationally plan investment directions. Distorted investment allocation which hinders the upgrading of industrial structure should be avoided. It is necessary to improve the efficiency of investment in fixed assets and give full play to the technological diffusion effect of fixed asset investment, which will increase the total factor productivity and promote the upgrading of industrial structure.

The government should rationally lay out the industry in the process of urbanization construction and deepen the industrial division of labor. The planning of industrial structure in urbanization should be comprehensively considered according to the natural resources, factor endowments and geographical location of each place. The local industries should be developed according to local conditions. In addition, the process of urbanization construction and promotion is also a process of upgrading the regional industrial structure and transforming production methods, which is not just the migration of the population at the formal level or the increase in population density and the number of towns, nor is it merely the expansion of the size of the town. It is not only an important task of the government but also a responsibility of the government in economic development to make long-sighted planning and design of urbanization development instead of the "population urbanization" and "land urbanization" merely in the conceptual sense. Only in this way can we promote the upgrading of industrial structure in the process of new urbanization construction in China.

5.3.3.3 Building a green financial system

At present, China is carrying out the construction of ecological civilization. The environmental regulation of enterprises is being continuously strengthened, energy-conservation, environmental-protection and high-tech industries are strongly supported and the green development of economy is strongly favored. Therefore, the demand for green finance is very strong in China. It is necessary to build a green financial system based on the existing financial development and give full play to the function of resource allocation of the capital market to improve environmental regulation in China and reduce the economic fluctuations and negative impacts brought about by environmental regulation. What's more, finance should serve the real economy. It plays a vital role in promoting the upgrading of industrial structure and supporting the construction of ecological civilization.

China should actively develop green credit. The green credit statistics system, green credit management system and evaluation system should be improved to give full play to the incentive mechanism of green credit for the development of green industry and the construction of green projects as well as the restraint mechanism for high pollution and high energy consumption industries. It is necessary to combine the environmental information of enterprises with credit information and construct an environmental information sharing mechanism so as to provide decision-making basis for banks to issue green credit.

The green securities market should be vigorously developed. It is important to improve the system of green securities issuance, information disclosure and rating evaluation. What's more, green enterprise financing should be actively supported, and relevant institutional investors should be encouraged to make green investments.

Absorbing social capital through public–private partnership (PPP) actively and supporting social capital to participate in environmental governance and green investment are excellent ways to increase environmental governance investment and promote the development of green industries.

China should improve the market of environmental rights and strengthen financial innovation. It is necessary to clearly define environmental property rights and provide a financial platform for environmental transactions to strengthen market mechanisms to solve environmental externalities. In addition, there is no doubt that financial instrument innovation and financial product innovation should be strengthened and financing tools should be enriched.

Green insurance should be developed. Green insurance products and services should be developed and provided. For example, it is possible to establish an insurance system related to the environment and climate change. The

Industrial structure upgrading 85

establishment of environmental risk monitoring, assessment and an early warning system is conducive to environmental risk management.

5.3.3.4 Improving foreign direct investment and foreign trade

Studies have shown that when foreign direct investment and foreign trade reach a certain level, it will help environmental regulation to promote the upgrading of industrial structure, which provides a theoretical basis for China to further expand its opening up and further increase foreign direct investment and foreign trade under the trend of strengthening environmental regulation.

The scale of foreign direct investment should be expanded and the quality of foreign direct investment should be improved. It is of vital importance to raise environmental regulation standards and strengthen environmental regulation. China should eliminate high-invasive, high-energy consumption foreign direct investment and other investment that is not conducive to China's economic restructuring to provide a good development environment for high-quality foreign direct investment. Generally, foreign direct investment with high-technology content, advanced management and strong R&D innovation ability tends to pay more attention to environmental quality, which will tend to be in areas with stricter environmental regulations. Therefore, the environmental regulation should be strengthened and the introduction of foreign direct investment should be closely combined with ecological environmental protection. Specifically, high-quality foreign direct investment should be introduced to give full play to the technology spillover effect of foreign direct investment; strengthen the supervision of foreign direct investment and strictly restrict the transfer of substandard foreign investment projects or industries among regions and to provide incentives to effectively promote the development of energy-saving and environmentally-friendly foreign direct investment enterprises. All these will help to promote the upgrading of China's industrial structure and economic restructuring.

China should adjust and optimize the structure of foreign trade. Although trade may affect the quality of the environment, foreign trade should not be reduced because of environmental problems. In fact, environmental regulations should be strengthened and effective strategies should be adopted to further expand foreign trade. We should try to achieve free trade while protecting the environment. In the context of economic globalization, the foreign trade structure of a country has an important impact on the country's industrial structure, and foreign trade is also a transmission path for environmental regulation to upgrade industrial structure. Therefore, it is essential to rationally and effectively adjust the structure of foreign trade. We should gradually reduce the foreign trade of resource-intensive products and increase the foreign trade of high-tech, energy-saving and environmentally-friendly products to increase the added value of foreign trade products.

5.3.3.5 Using environmental regulation tools rationally

China has a vast territory. The geographical, ecological, resource reserves and economic bases of the eastern, central and western regions are different. As a result, the environmental regulation standards and regulatory intensity are spatially heterogeneous. The level of technological innovation and innovation ability are also spatially heterogeneous. Therefore, local governments and relevant departments should adopt scientific plans to comprehensively assess local resource depletion, ecological damage and environmental pollution and then, according to local environmental capacity (environmental self-purification capacity), formulate reasonable environmental regulation standards. At the same time, in order to avoid macroeconomic fluctuations due to excessive environmental regulation intensity exceeding the company's ability to withstand it, it is necessary to formulate a long-term environmental regulation implementation plan and performance evaluation system, which should be implemented step by step. In addition, different types of environmental regulation tools should be used to effectively encourage enterprises to carry out environmental governance and eliminate speculation in environmental governance so as to promote environmental regulation to play an incentive or restraint role.

The environmental regulation tools should be used reasonably, and different types of environmental regulation tools should be effectively combined to increase environmental regulation intensity. Note that the regulations of different types of environmental regulation tools can promote the upgrading of industrial structure. There is no doubt that the greater the role of command-control environmental regulation tools and market-based environmental regulation tools, the more beneficial the environmental regulation is to promote industrial structure upgrades. Therefore, it is necessary to improve laws and regulations on environmental protection and strengthen the functions and responsibilities of government in environmental governance. Government investment in environmental governance should be increased, and environmental infrastructure should be actively constructed. The rapid development and innovation of market-based environmental regulation tools can enable environmental problems originally caused by market failure to be resolved by the market through the effective use of market-based environmental regulation. As for information disclosure–public participation environmental regulation tools, it is necessary to develop them, but they must be subject to certain laws, regulations or mechanisms to enable them to play an effective supervision role within a reasonable range to avoid the distortion of information or inappropriate behavior caused by them to disrupt the market. China should actively support the innovation of environmental regulation tools and enrich the types of environmental regulation tools to diversify environmental regulation tools.

5.3.3.6 Improving the environmental regulation system

At present, there is still a gap between China's environmental regulation system and those of developed countries. Although China's environmental regulation policy development and environmental governance work started in 1973, the stages of environmental regulation policy evolution have continued to move forward in a positive manner. However, it has not been highly valued in the specific practice process. The development of environmental regulation has been relatively slow, and so far, a sound environmental regulation system and a comprehensive information regulation database have not been established. China's environmental regulation work has only come to be highly valued with the more frequent occurrence of smog. Now that smog has begun to threaten people's health and life, China has begun to formulate the most stringent environmental regulation strategies and measures in history. Therefore, at this stage, in the process of increasing the intensity of environmental regulation, controlling haze and protecting resources and the environment, China must establish a sound environmental regulation system, so that all environmental protection and governance work is carried out within a sound environmental regulation system. Therefore, it provides perfect institutional arrangements and service for the construction and development of ecological civilization in China, and effectively solves the ecological and environmental problems in China.

The central government should establish a sound environmental regulation system operation mechanism and environmental regulation development plan. Local governments should combine the life cycle of local industry development with the current development stage to develop a suitable environmental regulation stage. Rational planning of arrangements for industrial transformation will accelerate the pace of upgrading industrial structure.

The central government should introduce a programmatic document on environmental regulation. Each local government will use this as a basic guideline and supplement it according to its own specific conditions. At the same time, this can also be one of the measures to solve the problem of "approaching the bottom line" of environmental regulation.

China should improve the resource price accounting system and reform the pricing mechanism of resources as soon as possible. Especially for energy resources, the depletion value should be fully considered in the price accounting system, which will help to save resources and protect the environment through market mechanisms.

A strict environmental regulation and supervision system should be established. A series of environmental regulation measures must involve the supervision system and conduct real-time supervision to effectively solve the emergencies and various non-standard problems or behaviors in environmental regulation.

A special organization should be set up in the environmental protection department to be responsible for the overall planning and leadership of the environmental regulation system to make the construction of the environmental regulation system work in an orderly and efficient manner.

Information on ecological environmental pollution and environmental regulation should be open and transparent. The public should have the right to know about the environmental conditions in which they live. The authoritative department should publicly disclose environmental information. On the one hand, it can make the public fully understand the environmental conditions of their own lives and raise their awareness of environmental protection. On the other hand, it can effectively avoid malicious attainments that are not in line with the facts. The establishment of a comprehensive database of environmental regulation information can help university research institutes to obtain comprehensive and effective information and data more easily in resource and environmental theory research. On the other hand, it also contributes to the construction and development of tools of information disclosure–public participation environmental regulation. Development of a comprehensive database is of great significance to the improvement of China's environmental regulation system.

5.3.3.7 Overcoming the middle-income trap

In the face of the development situation where the contradiction between resources and environment and economic growth is prominent, reasonable measures should be taken to rely on the market and innovation to improve industrial competitiveness, accelerate technological progress, enhance the endogenous driving force of economic growth, promote economic growth and cross the middle-income trap as soon as possible. Economic growth cannot be placed in a secondary position in order to control the environment. On the contrary, it is necessary to pay more attention to economic growth. Strengthening environmental regulation will raise the level of economic growth and promote the upgrading of industrial structure (Shi, 2017).

6 China's role in environmental globalization

Environmental globalization is an important feature of the era of globalization, which refers to the process and trend of internationalization and globalization of ecological and environmental issues. With the development of globalization, environmental problems have become more and more serious. Protecting the ecological environment has become an urgent and arduous task for the whole world. It requires the cooperation and efforts of all countries. In recent decades, some basic principles of behavioral norms related to global environmental governance have been formed, such as the principle of mutual cooperation, the principle of reciprocity of rights and responsibilities, the principle of inclusive growth, and so on. Although these principles have played a role in coordinating the relationship between the various actors in global environmental governance, environmental global governance still faces difficulties and obstacles, and it still has a long way to go.

The concept of environmental globalization emphasizes that in the context of the interconnected and interdependent nature of the world's ecological environment, the world should be turned into an organic whole from the perspective of ecological environment, with greater emphasis on eliminating the obstacles of solving environmental problems among countries in the world. It is necessary to actively participate in the global environment, strengthen international environmental cooperation and adopt international joint actions to maintain the stability, health and safety of the global ecosystem.

6.1 The main characteristics of environmental globalization

At present, the global ecological environment is characterized by eight major problems: (1) the global freshwater crisis – the challenge of scarce freshwater resources in the 21st century will outweigh all other challenges; (2) the global land crisis, especially the arable land crisis, is spreading globally; (3) the global forest crisis marks the transition from a period of global forest abundance to a period of global forest scarcity; (4) the global atmospheric crisis; (5) global warming poses a great threat to the survival of all mankind; (6) the destruction and depletion of the Earth's ozone layer; (7) the attenuation of the Earth's biodiversity and the accelerated speed of species extinction are important manifestations of the global ecological crisis; and (8) the transfer of hazardous wastes around the world.

From these eight problems, we can see that in the 21st century human beings face three types of prominent global environmental problems. The first is the destruction of global public resources, such as global warming and changes in the atmospheric environment caused by the greenhouse effect; the depletion and destruction of ozone layer causing environmental changes; and reduction in diversity of biological resources. Large-scale species extinctions cause changes in the basic ecological processes and life-sustaining systems of Earth's biosphere. Second is global transnational environmental pollution. A pollutant discharged by one country or region produces environmental pollution in other countries or regions, which is called transnational pollution, such as acid rain, sandstorm, sea pollution, public lake and international river pollution and so on. Third is the issue of "rent-seeking" in the global environment. In global resource-based rent-seeking activities, developed countries have carried out environmental rent-seeking activities for developing countries for their own economic interests and their own ecological environment. It is in the process of promoting economic globalization that developed countries have intensified the ecological crisis in developing countries, leading to the expansion of environmental problems from developed countries to developing countries.

The destruction of the ecological environment has expanded from a local hazard to an overall hazard, which has become a matter of life and death for all human beings, greatly threatening the security of human and non-human worlds. Ecological disasters in one country or region can endanger the ecological security of other countries and other regions. For example, carbon dioxide and other greenhouse gases emitted by one country or region can change the climate of another country or region, and may lead to global warming and sea level rise. It even affects the safety of the global ecosystem. For example, ecological destruction of the Amazon rain forest may pose regional or even global threats to the environment. The deterioration of the ecological environment not only harms human health and restricts economic development, but it also affects political, scientific and cultural development, and may affect economic security, political security and military security. In particular, some ecological problems will lead to conflicts and wars, leading to domestic and international violent conflicts. Therefore, the deterioration of the ecological environment has already posed a serious threat to international and national security. This makes ecological security or environmental safety an important foundation and basic guarantee for international and national security. The environmental problem is ultimately caused by human activities that are constantly transforming natural ecological conditions, and is influenced by factors such as human values, production methods and lifestyles. Under the conditions of modern science and technology, human beings have a strong force to influence or change the natural environment. The globalization of the world economy, international material production and global population growth have caused massive ecological and environmental damage. Therefore, the resolution of environmental problems requires global governance. As major global issues, environmental issues have a bearing on the global interests of the entire human race. It includes the common interests of mankind and all other life and the overall interests of the Earth's ecosystem. It has the characteristics of transcending country, nationality, region, social-political system and economic system, and directly determines and affects the interests of each country and nation. Therefore, it is impossible for some countries, nations and regions to solve global environmental problems alone. All countries, nations and regions in the world need to adopt a global consensus on the fundamental environmental problems in the world while solving their own environmental problems. All of us are working together, building a global partnership to solve this problem (Ding, 2013).

6.2 Environmental policy innovation in countries around the world

Under the background of environmental globalization, countries should be able to accurately and reasonably judge the nature of their own environmental issues in a timely manner and make trade-offs on policy tools and predict the outcomes of policy innovation for their complex and diverse environmental and ecological problems. However, they must also have a firm and determined will to solve environmental problems, grasp the direction of environmental innovation and overcome resistance to environmental innovation. At present, many countries have taken some measures to promote environmental policy innovation in light of their national conditions, policy foundations and social resources, becoming green countries and contributing their own efforts to protect the global ecological environment.

6.2.1 Prioritizing the establishment of environmental policy leader status

Countries that prioritize environmental policy leader status, based on a global perspective, grasp the development trend of international environmental policies, continue to promote national environmental policy reforms and formulate national and regional environmental policy plans for sustainable and green development as early as possible. They have established their positions as environmental policy leaders and use it to seek international competitive advantages. The ecological modernization model is based on the principle of equal emphasis on environmental protection and economic growth. It is a green development concept and strategy that has been successfully explored by the EU and its core countries. The Federal Republic of Germany first proposed and practiced the ecological modernization model. Professor Martin Jenicke of the Environmental Policy Research Center of Free University of Berlin proposed the concept of "ecological modernization" for the first time in 1982, and it was gradually implemented by the German government as the basic state policy of the ruling party. The Netherlands has also actively implemented a sustainable development strategy. Since 1988, it has continuously launched its own National Environmental Policy Plan (NEPP), emphasizing the institutional innovation of green development. The advanced environmental policy innovations in Germany and the Netherlands have produced strong "overflow" and "spread" effects. For example, Germany's power grid repurchase policy has been adopted by more than 30 countries, and the environmental policy planning of the Netherlands has influenced the formulation of sustainable development national strategies of more than 100 countries. The EU has continuously formulated and implemented six Environmental Action Plans (EAPs) since 1973, making the green economy and technological advantages the political strength of the EU in global climate change negotiations. The EU and its core countries have also become leaders in formulating global climate change strategies since the mid-1990s.

6.2.2 Improving the organizational system

These countries focus on the integration of national environmental policy innovation organizations and environmental protection capacity building and governance system reform. They provide an organizational system foundation for the coordinated promotion of environmental innovation policies and t/he comprehensive integration of environmental governance. Green development countries have experienced the pain of the reform of the integration, restructuring and empowerment of environmental protection departments. They all focus on promoting green development by strengthening environmental protection functions and increasing enforcement of environmental policies. For example, France created department of nature and environmental protection in 1971, and subsequently established CIDD, the National Advisory Council on Sustainable Development,

Économique, Social et Environnemental (CESE) and the National Committee for Public Debate. These organizations are responsible for formulating and implementing national strategies for sustainable development and expanding the environmental policy power of citizens to participate in green development. In 2007, the cabinet reorganization led the environmental protection department to merge the key functions of some ministries, such as the Ministry of Ecology, the Ministry of Energy, and the Ministry of Sustainable Development, and the Regional and Planning Committee. It has a high administrative level and management authority in the national ministries. In the 1990s, the United Kingdom launched sectoral integration and institutional reform with sustainable development as the core to solve the functional conflicts of environmental management and the fragmentation of environmental laws and policies, and to promote the two-level integration of environmental management functions and environmental policy laws. On the one hand, after a long and tortuous process, Environmental Agency was established in 1996 to concentrate the environmental protection and pollution prevention functions that were originally dispersed in many regulatory agencies in a unified institution. On the other hand, the "Greening Government Initiative" was launched in 1990 (renamed "Sustainable Development in Government" in 2001) and is committed to building an integrated government centered on sustainable development and pursuing sustainable development based on environmental governance integration.

6.2.3 Promoting the implementation of environmental innovation policies

These countries use a variety of policy tools, such as comprehensive administrative tools and market mechanisms, to inspire green technology innovation and develop a green economy. They encourage enterprises to internalize environmental costs and promote the implementation and diffusion of environmental innovation policies. In order to promote the concept of energy conservation and emission reduction from "the one who pollutes pays" to "the one who is environmentally friendly benefits", the EU countries have introduced many comprehensive environmental tax incentives such as fiscal and taxation policies, administrative means, market mechanisms, etc. They encourage companies to pay attention to environmental interests, internalize environmental costs and shift from end-of-pipe treatment to prevention. They are actively involved in global environmental governance and provide economic and technical assistance to environmental governance in developing countries. Sweden, which is committed to building a green welfare state, is one of the countries in the world that have the most stringent environmental protection laws and use the strongest economic means in environmental protection. According to the 2004 assessment by the Organisation for Economic Co-operation and Development (OECD), Sweden has implemented about 70 market-based instruments, the most striking of which is the introduction of environmental taxes and green tax reforms such as carbon dioxide taxes, sulfur taxes, nitrogen oxide taxes, natural gravel taxes, and landfill taxes from the early 1990s to the beginning of the 21st century. At the same time, in order to alleviate the tax burden on the energy sector caused by the new environmental taxes, the original energy tax of the industrial sector is exempted or reduced so as to achieve the dual dividends of pollution suppression and financial benefits. Austria's ultimate mobilization-oriented environmental policy is quite strict and efficient, providing a strong corporate support system for early terminal technologies and current clean technologies. The Japanese government has adopted comprehensive environmental measures and long-term plans to reform the industrial structure and fund infrastructure construction, They encourage private investment in energy-saving technologies and low-carbon energy technology innovation. Japan continues to invest in fossil energy emission reduction technology and coal-fired power plant flue gas desulfurization technology and equipment, forming a leading international flue gas desulfurization and environmental protection industry.

6.2.4 Enhancing legislation and management of environmental policies

These countries continue to improve the legislative and management capacity of environmental policies to provide legal system guarantees for environmental policy innovation. The EU attaches great importance to strengthening its environmental functions in the process of integration. It is precisely by continuously improving environmental policy legislation and promoting environmental cooperation actions that it has become a global model for green development and environmental governance. The 1972 Paris Summit was an important turning point for the European Community to establish its environmental policy and legal system. It has successively adopted six environmental action programs, urging the focus of environmental policy from environmental protection to environmental integration and sustainable development and the direction from end-of-pipe treatment to integrated product policy. It made EU environmental policy a model for international environmental cooperation. Germany was one of the earliest countries in Europe to start paying attention to environmental issues. In 1972, Germany passed the first environmental protection law, the Waste

Disposal Act (*AbfG*). In the early 1990s, environmental protection was written into the Basic Law (*das Grundgesetz*). Germany has the most complete and specific environmental legislation and the most stringent environmental standards. There are more than 8000 environmental laws and regulations in the German federal and state governments, and about 400 relevant regulations of the EU are implemented. In France, the formulation of the Integrated Environmental Policy and Consultation Act (*Grenelle*) marked a major innovation in French environmental legislation from centralized legislation to negotiated legislation, and from individual legislation to policy and planning legislation. The highly integrated and one-stop legislative approach in France was conducive to achieving the overall "greening" of the legislative system, which provides a reference for global environmental policy legislative innovation.

6.2.5 Strengthening civic education for green development

These countries actively cultivate NGOs (non-governmental organizations) and the public who support environmental policy innovation. They are committed to strengthening cultural development and civic education for green development, providing a solid social foundation and mobilization for environmental policy innovation. European and American countries have provided relaxed development space for environmental NGOs, such as the Friends of the Earth, Greenpeace, the Wilderness Society, the World Wide Fund for Nature and other environmental groups. These countries provide expert advice and decision-making directions to environmental decision-makers through various formal or informal channels. The environmental movement has become more professional and institutionalized, and the focus of environmental movements has shifted from local pollution issues to global environmental issues. It has played an important role in mobilizing the public for Western social environmental policy reforms. Japan's environmental innovation not only pays attention to government management model innovation, but also emphasizes environmental education and public participation. Japan enacts environmental education as a basic policy. It not only carries on the general systematic environmental education to the public through the Environmental Education Act, but also mandates specific education through special legislation. For example, Article 25 of the Basic Law of the Environment, Article 27 of the Basic Law on Promoting the Formation of a Circular Society and Article 8 of the Law on Promotion of the Utilization of Renewable Resources make specific provisions on national environmental resource awareness education, environmental resource education and learning systems. At the same time, Japan has provided the public with several ways to receive announcements, submit opinions, participate in hearings, understand the environmental conditions, provide feedback and participate in environmental supervision.

6.2.6 Adhering to the national environmental policy reform

National environmental policy reform is not realized in the short term. It is a long-term and gradual process. It is necessary to overcome various obstacles in policy resources, economic structure, institutional framework and legal traditions, and to pay considerable cost in terms of economy, efficiency and time. As a result, the status of the green development countries will change and fluctuate. For example, the EU is the main force to promote environmental policy innovation in its member states. However, there are significant differences in the cost, benefit and success of "legislative competition" in the specific practice of formulating and adopting environmental innovation policies and standards due to significant differences in geographical environmental conditions, economic development levels, industrial structure, and laws and regulations. In 1990, the EU issued Free Access to Information in an open, negotiated environmental law enforcement innovation model to clarify the citizens' right to know about the environment and government responsibility. Austria is an EU country with high environmental awareness and strict environmental measures. Its consensus-oriented, consultative and discussion-oriented environmental policy formulation path has strong advantages. However, Austria no longer intends to establish its image as a "pioneer", but rather to reduce the importance of environmental affairs. It is only willing to follow the path of EU environmental policies. In 1970, the massive Earth Day campaign broke out in the United States in protest against the increasingly serious industrial pollution. That was regarded as a historical starting point for integrating environmental issues into the global vision. It directly promoted environmental legislation in many countries, and was also known as the beginning of the modern environmental movement. However, the United States has not been able to maintain its environmental policy innovation. In order to control greenhouse gas emissions, the international community introduced the Kyoto Protocol in 1997. For the first time, it was legally determined that the total greenhouse gas emissions of all industrialized countries must be reduced by 5.2% from 1990 to 2012. According to the agreement, the EU needed to reduce emissions by 8%, the United States by 7%, and Japan by 6%. However, the United States declared a fatal flaw in the Kyoto Protocol in March 2001 and unilaterally withdrew from the climate agreement. This is because the Kyoto Protocol and its directive greenhouse gas emissions were not in line with the will of the United States. At the same time, the United States has actively formulated a series of policies and laws to promote the development of low-carbon industries, focusing on enhancing the core competitiveness of the green energy sector (Shu, 2016).

6.3 The dilemma faced by the governance system

National environmental initiatives have contributed to the governance of environmental globalization to a large extent, but enormous difficulties remain. The dilemma is closely related to the sharing of the earth's resources and is a manifestation of the tragedy of the commons. With the ebb and flow of global economic power and the changing pattern of interests, it is more difficult to balance the interests of all parties. Negotiations on the global environment have become more difficult, and global environmental governance has entered a difficult stage. The real dilemma of the global environmental governance system is mainly reflected in the following aspects.

6.3.1 Conflicts in the environmental globalization governance system

There are many internal contradictions in the global environmental governance system, which makes it difficult to form a unified external governance force. The effectiveness of global environmental governance depends on the strength of governance, and external governance depends on the internal unity and coordination within the system. It is difficult for the global environmental governance system to form external governance synergy due to the divergence of interests, different values and the pursuit of power. It is mainly manifested in the differences between the developed countries and developing countries on the causes of ecological crises and the division of responsibility for environmental issues. Although developed countries have advantages in terms of technology, capital and management experience in global environmental governance, they tend to be conservative and passive in specific actions. Some countries refuse to acknowledge their historical responsibility for environmental pollution, and delay or even evade their aid commitments. Developing countries are faced with the dual tasks of developing the economy and protecting the environment. It is impossible to sacrifice development for environmental protection, and the help of developed countries is needed to achieve coordination between the two. At the same time, there are contradictions within the developed countries. In order to compete for the dominance of global environmental governance, developed countries have differences in the setting of governance models and mechanisms. For example, in the context of global climate governance, the active promotion of the EU, the negative response of the United States and the wait-and-see attitudes of countries such as Canada and Japan have formed a stark contrast. Developing countries also have differences on some issues of global environmental governance. China, India and several Latin American countries insist that developed countries bear historical responsibility, while some small island states propose that developed countries and large developing countries need to increase the intensity of emission reduction. Incentives should be established for all countries. The contradictions within the global environmental governance system make global cooperation difficult to advance.

6.3.2 Insufficient support for environmental globalization governance

Insufficient support for global environmental governance has limited its effectiveness. Global environmental governance is a systematic project that needs a large amount of funds, technology, talents and other factors as well as a series of supporting reforms and services. An example of capital may be helpful. According to international experience, when the proportion of investment in addressing environmental pollution is 1–1.5% of GDP, the trend of environmental degradation can be controlled. When it reaches 2–3%, environmental quality can be improved (Huang & Ye, 2016). However, most developing countries and underdeveloped countries are lagging behind in economic development. Their limited resources are focused on developing the economy. There is a serious lack of funds, technology and talents for environmental governance. In addition, the design of the statistical system for sustainable development is imperfect, and it lacks data, making it difficult to conduct regular testing and evaluation. An authoritative global governance body is needed to guide the optimal allocation of resources for international environmental protection and to provide more elements for environmental governance in underdeveloped countries. Although the current international environmental governance negotiations have formed a relatively broad consensus on the finance, technology and other aid responsibilities of developed countries, there is no coercive or binding force in the specific implementation process. Therefore, many countries have not fulfilled the agreement, and the process of assistance is fragmented. As a non-profit organization, the global environmental governance institution has limited funding sources and financing methods. The technological innovation capability of environmental protection is insufficient, and there is a lack of corresponding talents who understand technology and environmental management. As a result, the daily global environmental governance capacity is unsustainable and has little effect. It can only be consolidated and emphasized by periodic global environmental conferences.

6.3.3 Limited subjects in environmental globalization governance

The traditional body of global environmental governance has inhibited innovation. The initial global environmental governance system was based on neoliberal concepts and was driven and controlled by Western countries. With the rise of emerging countries and the declining influence of Western countries, coupled with the continued spread of environmental pollution, the governance model dominated by Western countries has gradually shifted to a model that serves the interests of the global public. However, it has not fundamentally changed the dominant position of governance in developed countries. No matter who takes the lead, the main body of global environmental governance is based on government departments. Although a number of NGOs and companies are involved, their role is limited – only the right to make recommendations, and the setting of environmental governance systems is determined by the government organization. For example, the focus of the Rio +20 summit was to reform the institutional framework for sustainable development, but the negotiators were gathered in intergovernmental organizations such as the United Nations Environment Programme (UNEP), the Commission on Sustainable Development (CSD) and the Economic and Social Council (ECOSOC). NGOs and businesses were more concerned with financing sustainable development than with having a say in key institutional design. This single global environmental governance approach excludes private participation in governance from the global governance system and inhibits innovation and vitality of private governance. As a result, global environmental governance has only been adjusted within the established model and framework, making it difficult to achieve substantive breakthroughs. The scope of global environmental governance should be extended to NGOs, multinational corporations and additional international institutions. It should recognize both intergovernmental cooperation and the cooperation among NGOs, global international organizations and other groups. Only in this way can the current imbalance of power in global environmental governance be eliminated and the dominance of some powerful countries checked. Finally, global participation in environmental governance will be realized (Huang & Ye, 2016).

In sum, the development of environmental protection in global governance lags far behind the level of economic globalization, and the problem clearly cannot be resolved by simple communication between governments. Attempts to downplay global environmental problems are pointless as the consequences become clear. A relatively balanced global governance structure among global markets, global civil society and global coalition governments should be established to achieve true ecological democracy. Only when strong and weak countries are equal to each other in the face of environmental problems and human beings and other non-human world can live in harmony with the concept of "harmonious world" can we alleviate and solve the environmental problems of globalization (Ding, 2013).

6.4 Suggestions on China's participation in global environmental governance

The following are suggestions on how China can successfully participate in global environmental governance.

6.4.1 Recognizing the situation and changing the way of thinking

At present, China's own environmental problems have a great impact on global environmental issues. Western countries are very concerned about the impact of China's development on the global environment and resources. Therefore, China's environmental governance faces severe challenges in the context of global environmental governance. In the 1950s and 1960s, Western countries experienced serious environmental pollution problems. However, after investing a large amount of manpower, material resources and financial resources, environmental pollution was effectively controlled and the environmental quality was fundamentally improved. At present, the focus of environmental governance has shifted from pollution control to a global climate change response. However, China's environmental protection work is significantly different from that of Western developed countries in terms of goals. The mandatory indicators included in the national ecological environmental protection plan during the 13th Five-Year Plan period involve the number of days with excellent air quality at the prefecture level and above; the unqualified concentration of fine particulate matter at the prefecture level and above; the proportion of surface water that is better than Class III; the proportion of surface water inferior to Class V; the safe utilization rate of contaminated cultivated land; and the total amount of chemical oxygen demand, ammonia nitrogen, sulfur dioxide and nitrogen oxide pollutants. However, climate change, ozone layer protection, biodiversity, transboundary water pollution and other global environmental issues which are currently of wide concern by the international community are not among the priority treatment areas. Therefore, in the process of participating in global environmental governance, China needs to fully recognize its environmental stage and position. At the same time, efforts should be made to increase China's participation in other global environmental governance hotspot issues.

6.4.2 Participating in the formulation of environmental governance rules

Participation in global environmental governance can generally be divided into three stages: first, to be familiar with existing rules and strictly abide by them; second, to be proficient in using existing rules to actively protect your rights and interests; finally, to be able to lead or participate in rule-making for your own benefit. At present, China is still at the end of the first phase and the beginning of the second phase. At the G20 Summit in Hangzhou in 2016, President Xi Jinping clearly proposed to implement *Transforming Our World: The 2030 Agenda for Sustainable Development*. He pointed out that China should rely on an innovation-driven development strategy and be an "action team". China is supposed to participate in the work of global environmental governance as a responsible major country. The "Five Development Concepts" followed by the 13th Five-Year Plan for the Protection of Ecological Environment have clearly set requirements for economic development, social development and environmental protection. This is the three core aspects of *Transforming Our World: The 2030 Agenda for Sustainable Development*. The Overall Layout of "Five in One" of economic construction, political construction, cultural construction, social construction and ecological civilization construction is also consistent with the core connotation of *Transforming Our World: The 2030 Agenda for Sustainable Development*. It can be said that, in this sense, China will promote the two major international and domestic situations, and take environmental protection as a way to implement China's peaceful development path, building a new type of international relations, with cooperation and win-win as the core; establishing a "Community of Shared Future for Mankind" and emphasizing the "Belt and Road Initiative". International strategic thinking is crucial to safeguarding China's national interests and enhancing its international voice.

6.4.3 Improving the environmental governance system in China

Under the new trend of global environmental governance and the objective requirements of China's active participation in promoting global environmental governance, it is necessary to solve current environmental management problems such as the division of China's administrative departments, each of which only accomplishes its own goals and lacks coordination. The shortcomings of the current environmental protection management system should be addressed, and the integration of ecological and environmental protection functions and related resources should be strengthened. An ecological environment management system with unified functions, coordinated operation and high efficiency should be established. In terms of improving the legal system of environmental protection, it is necessary to regulate the behavior of people and enterprises and to reduce the impact of production and consumption activities on the environment by designing a complete and thorough environmental legal system with strong operability and timely adjustment. In terms of human resource construction, the number, quality and technical support of China's personnel participating in global environmental governance are not in line with current needs. Great efforts should be made in capital, technical capacity and personnel construction. In terms of science and technology support, participation in global environmental governance must act in accordance with international thinking and follow the inherent laws of global and environmental governance. In the past few years, China has invested a lot in climate change, but its investment in other areas of global environmental governance have been quite limited. In the future, special research should be carried out promptly to develop scientific strategies for China to actively participate in global environmental governance. In terms of public participation, it is important to give full play to the positive role of China's environmental NGOs in global environmental governance and to make use of the discourse power and influence of NGOs to reflect China's unique national conditions and interests in global environmental governance. However, China should also actively promote public participation in environmental governance and publicize environmental information. The public's right to know about the environment should be guaranteed, and relevant institutional arrangements for public participation in environmental protection should be provided (Liu & Xu, 2017).

6.4.4 Exploring a green development path with Chinese characteristics

China should choose the path of environmental policy innovation suitable for China's social and cultural context, and provide global environmental governance with environmental innovation technologies, environmental innovation products, environmental innovation policies and environmental policy standards originated in China. Over the past 40 years of reform and opening up, China has made huge investments to improve the ecological environment. At the same time, China has continuously carried out policy formulation and environmental legislation and fulfilled its commitments to participate in global environmental governance and safeguard global ecological security. These initiatives have been highly valued by the international community. For example, in its 1997 report *Clear Water, Blue Skies: China's Environment in the New Century*, the World Bank highly praised the "total amount control" and "green engineering" of China. The World Bank pointed out that "many countries only commit to vague environmental protection tasks, while China has put forward a clear set of measurable goals". The green development paths adopted by different countries in the world are diverse. For example, the Philippines and Germany have adopted a comprehensive multidimensional path, Cameroon has adopted an interdepartmental path, Canada and the United Kingdom have chosen a sectoral path and Mexico has taken the path of integrating sustainable development into other existing plans. China must choose a green development strategy path that is suitable for its own environmental resource base, economic and political system, public environmental appeal and environmental policy resources. This is because "the choice of strategic path usually reflects the long-term institutional framework conditions, policy culture and regulatory ladder of a country . . . the state must adopt a strategic approach that meets its specific needs and is compatible with the conditions of its institutional framework – there is no single recipe" (Shu, 2016).

In addition, the status of representative countries in environmental policy innovation will change. The United States, Japan and Sweden were the trendsetters in the 1970s, while Germany, Norway, the Netherlands and other EU countries became the emerging countries in environmental policy innovation in the 1980s and 1990s. Although China is faced with extremely severe environmental governance problems, it has its own unique advantages in environmental policy innovation and is expected to grow into an emerging country with environmental policy innovation on the path of green development in the 21st century. First, China has relatively complete environmental policies and legislation. The Environmental Protection Law of the People's Republic of China (trial) was promulgated at the beginning of reform and opening up in 1979. In 1983, the second National Conference on Environmental Protection declared that environmental protection was a basic national policy. In 2005, the State Council issued the Decision of the State Council on Implementing the Scientific Outlook on Development and Strengthening Environmental Protection, which placed environmental protection in a more important strategic position. Since the 18th National Congress of the Communist Party of China (CPC), it has further promoted the construction of ecological civilization systems such as the farmland protection system, the system of paid use of resources, the ecological compensation system, the accountability system and the system of compensation for environmental damage. These have improved the target system, assessment methods and reward and punishment mechanisms for green development. Second, the CPC is determined to pursue a green development path.

The report of the 18th National Congress of the CPC clearly put the construction of ecological civilization in the prominent position of a national development strategy, stressing that it must be integrated into all aspects and the whole process of economic, political, cultural and social development. In 2015, the green development strategy was included in the 13th Five-Year Plan, so it is expected to form a good positive synergy between top-down environmental policy reform decision-making and implementation and bottom-up public environmental policy reform demands. Third, China's development of new energy industries such as optical fiber, wind power and solar energy has almost kept pace with the developed countries. It provides a technical basis and comparative advantage for China's participation in global competition of green economy and green development cooperation. It is expected to provide global environmental governance with environmental innovation technologies, products produced by environmental innovation technologies, environmental innovation policies and environmental policy standards originating in China. "China, as the world's largest emerging economy, should also become an advocate, innovator and frontrunner of this green industrial revolution" (Hu, & Zhou, 2014).

However, China must clarify the direction of environmental policy innovations in the future. On the basis of the relatively complete and mature environmental policy legislation, China should focus on strengthening the concrete system construction of green development and ecological civilization, as well as the implementation effect and efficiency of environmental innovation policies. In addition, China should pay more attention to the environment and integrate it into economic decision-making, institutional reform and technological innovation. Innovation and implementation of comprehensive policies should be strengthened. China should also grasp the new changes in global environmental governance. China must not only establish emission reduction targets and commitments to undertake global environmental responsibility, but also understand that although environmental protection and green development policy innovations are prone to significant results in the early stage, the resistance of interest groups and the difficulty of reforms in the later stages are both difficult. Therefore, it is necessary to persistently and firmly promote environmental policy innovation to prove its environmental effectiveness and environmental competitiveness. As Fox and Miller put it, "A successful public policy will change the repetitive practices, which are the repetitive patterns of behavior that constitute our cultural habits and assumptions" (Fox & Miller, 2002).

In short, China should give full play to its institutional advantages. It should be clarified that green development is an important way to accelerate the construction of a resource-conserving and environment-friendly society and to build China into a moderately prosperous society in an all-round way. It is the only way for the transformation and upgrading of emerging countries. China should increase the R&D investment in independent innovation of green technologies and actively promote the green transition of domestic industries. A green technology transfer mechanism with developed countries should be improved. It is necessary to strengthen international cooperation in environmental governance and steadily promote the construction of a beautiful China. Finally, a new pattern of modernization in the harmonious development of man and nature will be formed. We should follow the basic principle of global environmental governance of "common but differentiated responsibilities" and make new contributions to global ecological security.

References

Baidu Encyclopedia. https://baike.baidu.com/item/中国水污染/15435962?fr=aladdin

Baidu Library. https://wenku.baidu.com/view/1870dc7c842458fb770bf78a65296 47d27283487.html

Cao, Hongyan. Remarkable Progress Has Been Made in Ecological and Environmental Protection in China. *Economic Daily*, 2015–10–10(4).

Chen, Jianpeng. Retrospect and Prospect of China's Environmental Governance in the Past 40 Years. *China Economic Times*, 2018–12–10(5).

Ding, Shan. Thoughts on Environmental Globalization. *Academic Research*, 2013(2): 66–70.

Fox, Charles & Miller, Hugh. Postmodern Public Administration——Toward Discourse. Beijing: China Renmin University Press, 2002." in front of "Han, Xiaohui. The Implementation Dilemma and Institutional Response of China's Environmental Policy. Journal of Fujian Provincial Committee Party School of CPC 2017(9):64–70.

Han, Xiaohui. The Implementation Dilemma and Institutional Response of China's Environmental Policy. *Journal of Fujian Provincial Committee Party School of CPC*, 2017(9):64–70.

He, Shaoyue. An Analysis of the New Developments of China's Environmental Policies since the 18th CPC National Congress. *Thinking*, 2017, 43(1):93–100.

Hu, Angang & Zhou Shaojie. Green Development: Functional Definition, Mechanism Analysis and Development Strategy. *China Population, Resources and Environment*, 2014, 24(01):14–20.

Hu, Jintao. *Firmly March on the Path of Socialism with Chinese Characteristics and Strive to Complete the Building of a Moderately Prosperous Society in All Respects: Report at the 18th National Congress of the CPC*. Beijing: People's Public House, 2012.

Huang, Jing. *Study on the Relationship and Influence Mechanism of Environmental Pollution and Economic Sustainable Development*. Hunan University, 2010.

Huang, Xinhuan & Ye, Qi. The Construction and Strategic Choice of Global Environmental Governance System. *Review of Economic Research*, 2016(16):4–11.

Liu, Dong & Xu, Mengjia. Study on the New Dynamic of Global Environmental Governance and Strategies of Improving China's Participation. *Environmental Protection*, 2017, 45(6):60–63.

Liu, Zhengyan & Li, Zhong. A Preliminary Study on Regional Differentiated Environmental Policy in China. *China Economic & Trade Herald*, 2018(21):70–72.

References

Ministry of Ecology and Environment of the People's Republic of China. *Bulletin of China's Ecological Environment*, 2017: 4–55.

National Bureau of Statistics. *China Statistical Yearbook*. Beijing: China Statistics Press, 2008–2017.

Ruan, 2011. www.cn-hw.net/html/32/200904/10074.html

Ruan, Xin. The Status Quo of Solid Waste Pollution in China and Its Countermeasures. *Modern Science*, 2011(2):34.

Shi, Lele. *Research on the Influence of Environmental Regulation on China's Industrial Structure Upgrading*. Xinjiang University, 2017.

Shu, Shaofu. Environmental Policy Innovation of Green Development: International Mirror and Enlightenment. *Reform*, 2016(3):102–109.

Sustainable Development Strategy Research Group of Chinese Academy of Sciences. *China Sustainable Development Report 2013*. Beijing: Science Press, 2013.

Wang, Lei. *Research on the Influence of Environmental Regulation on the Optimization and Upgrade of China's Industrial Structure*. Yunnan University of Finance and Economics, 2018.

Wang, Linsheng, Le, Meiqing & Zhang, Taisen. *Introduction to Environmental Chemistry*. Shanghai: East China Normal University Press, 2006.

Xi, Jinping. *Secure a Decisive Victory in Building a Moderately Prosperous Society in All Respects and Strive for the Great Success of Socialism with Chinese Characteristics for a New Era: Report at the 19th National Congress of the CPC*. Beijing: People's Public House, 2017:10.

Xu, Qiuli. Analysis on the Status Quo of Air Pollution in China and Its Prevention and Control Measures. *Theoretical Research in Urban Construction*, 2018(14):137.

Yang, Honggang. *Research on the Implementation Effect and Selection of Environmental Policy Tools in China*. Fudan University, 2009.

Zhang, Kunmin, Wen, Zongguo & Peng, Liying. China's Environmental Policy: Formation, Characteristics and Evaluation. *Compilation of Dissertation of China Association of Plant Engineering*, 2007:23.

Zhang, Xu. The Urgency and Necessity of Environmental Pollution Control in China. *Brand*, 2014(10):53.

Zhong, Jie. *Research on the Enforcement and Synergy of China's Environmental Policy*. Yanshan University, 2016.

Zhou, Shengxian. The Development Course and Effect of Environmental Protection in China. *Environmental Protection*, 2013, 41(14):10–13.

Zhou, Yuan, Zhang, Xiaodong, Zhao, Yun, Chen, Luyi & Xue, Lan. Industrial Development and Environmental Performance under the Regulation of Green Governance. *China Population, Resources and Environment*, 2018, 28(9):82–92.

Index

Note: Page numbers in *italics* indicate figures and in **bold** indicate tables on the corresponding pages.

Action Plan for Prevention and Control of Atmospheric Pollution 37
Action Plan for Prevention and Control of Water Pollution 33
added value of products 71–72
air pollution 5–6, 13–14
automobile emissions 5–6, *6*

backward capacity, eliminating 80–81
biosphere destruction 90

centralized pollution control system 29
China: environmental globalization role of (*see* environmental globalization); environmental policy of (*see* environmental policy); exploring a green development path for 102–105; impact of pollution on industrial development in 13–15; industrial development and ecological damage in 9–10; pollution in 5–8, *6–8*; rapid economic growth of 4; sustainable development strategies in 4–5
China Sustainable Development Report 18
Chinese Academy of Sciences 13
Clear Water, Blue Skies: China's Environment in the New Century 103
command-control environmental policy tools 28–29
Commission on Sustainable Development (CSD) 99

Communist Party of China (CPC) 1, 16, 17, 56, 103
comparative advantages 75–77
competitive advantages 75–77
Convention on International Trade in Endangered Species of Wild Fauna and Flora 9
cultural industries 77–78

desertified land 9–10
differentiated environmental policy 31–35
discharge permit system 24, 28–29, 32–33

early warning systems 54
ecological damage and industrial development 9–10
ecological refugees 10
Economic and Social Council (ECOSOC) 99
education expenditures 83
emissions trading system 29
environmental globalization 89; adhering to national environmental policy reform and 96–97; dilemma faced by governance system in 97–100; enhancing legislation and management of environmental policies and 94–95; environmental policy innovations in countries around the world and 91–97; improving the organizational system and 92–93; main characteristics of

89–91; prioritizing establishment of environmental policy leader status and 91–92; promoting the implementation of environmental innovation policies 93–94; strengthening civic education for green development 95–96; suggestions on China's participation in global environmental governance and 100–105
environmental governance 36; countermeasures for implementation of environmental policy 48–56; effectiveness of China's 36–38; environmental globalization and 97–100; improving China's 101–102; multiple political policies and unclear rights and responsibilities in 39; policy defects and implications for sustainable development 39–42; suggestions for China's participation in global 100–105; sustainable development and 42–48
environmental impact assessment system 28
environmental information disclosure 29
environmental labeling system 30–31
environmental legal system 51–53
environmental planning system 28
environmental policy 1–3, 16; basic characteristics of China's 17–18; changes in 30–31; countermeasures for implementation of 48–56; in countries around the world 91–97; deviations in implementation of 39–41; differential development and differentiated 31–35; enlightenment stage of **19**; environmental management stage of 22–27, **25**; environmental system construction stage of 20, **20–21**; establishing leader status in 91–92; evolution of industrial development and 18–27, **19–23, 25**; imperfect assessment system for 46; imperfect supervision mechanism for 46–47; improving the mechanism of 50–51; insufficient interaction of supervisors of 41–42; insufficient selectivity of tools in 47–48; lack of consistency in implementation of 43–46; lack of continuity in implementation

of 41; large-scale environmental management stage of 20–22, **22–23**; low efficiency of tools in 42; macro level 17, 82–88; meso level 17, 72–81; micro level 17–18, 70–72; promoting institutional innovation 48–50; recommendations for 69–88; sustainable development and 42–48; sustainable developments and defects in 39–42; tools for 27–31
environmental pollution liability insurance 29
environmental protection target responsibility 29
environmental regulation 64–69; improving 86–88
environmental technology 53–55, 70–71
excess, eliminating 80–81

financial instruments 72, 82–83; building a green financial system and 84–85
foreign direct investment 85–86
foreign trade 85–86
forest reserves 37–38
fragmentation 42–43

globalization *see* environmental globalization
governance *see* environmental governance
Great Western Development Strategy 15
green financial system 84–85
Guidance on Implementation of Action Plan for Water Pollution Prevention and Implementation of Regional Differentiated Environmental Access 33

hazardous waste *see* noxious waste pollution
hollowing out of industries, prevention of 78–80

industrial chain 74–75
industrial development: differentiated 31–35; ecological damage due to 9–10, *10*; environmental regulation and 64–69; evolution of environmental policy and 18–27, **19–23, 25**; impact

of pollution on 13–15; industrial structure and 57–64, **59–60**, **61**, *62*, **63**; policy tools and 27–31; regional pollution due to 10–11, **12**, *12–13*
industrial structure 57; development of 57–62, **59–61**, *62*, **63**; industrial development and 57–64; insufficient labor productivity and 67–68; insufficient quality and efficiency of upgrading in 68–69; policy recommendations for 69–88; regional upgrading in 62–64, **63**
information disclosure-public participation in environmental regulation 54–55, 66–67
institutional innovation, promotion of 48–50
investment, foreign direct 85–86
ISO14000 environmental series standard 30

Jenicke, M. 92

labor productivity, insufficient 67–68; improving 81
Leading Group of Ecological Civilization 49–50
Leading Group of Ecological Civilization Construction 49
legal system, environmental 51–53

macro-environmental policy 17; recommendations for 82–88
market-based environmental regulation 64–66
Marxist ideology 17
meso-environmental policy 17; recommendations for 72–81
micro-environmental policy 17–18; recommendations for 70–72
middle-income trap 88
Ministry of Environmental Protection 49–50
monitoring, environmental 54
moral education 28

National Environmental Protection Agency/Bureau 13, 26
National Environmental Protection Conference 18–19
noxious waste pollution 7–8, *8*, 14

obligation standard 30
Organisation for Economic Co-operation and Development (OECD) 94

policy tools *see* environmental policy
pollution: air 5–6, *6*, 13–14; differential development and regional 10–11, **12**, *12–13*; impact on industrial development 13–15; noxious waste 7–8, *8*, 14; severity of 5–8, *6–8*; solid waste 14–15; water 6–7, *7*, 14
public participation in environmental protection 55–56, 66–67; in different countries 95–96
public resources, destruction of global 90

Qu Geping 4

regional pollution 10–11, **12**, *12–13*; sluggish upgrading and 68
regional upgrading in industrial structure 62–64, **63**
regulation, environmental 64–69; improving 86–88
rent-seeking activities 90

service industry 79–80
sewage charging system 29
Shanghai Academy of Public Measurement 14
soil erosion 9
solid waste 14–15
species extinction 9
standard of right 30
subsidies 29
supervision of environmental policy implementation 41–42
sustainable development: fragmentation and lack of coordination among formulators in 42–43; policy defects and implications for 39–42; strategies for 4–5

taxes, environmental 32, 47, 50–51
technology, environmental 53–55, 70–71
total factor productivity 73–74
Transforming Our World: The 2030 Agenda for Sustainable Development 101

United Nations Conference on the Human Environment 17, 18
United Nations Environment Programme (UNEP) 99
urbanization 38, 83

value chain 74–75

water pollution 6–7, 7, 14
Water Pollution Prevention Action 33

World Bank 13, 27
World Health Organization (WHO) 6
World Trade Organization (WTO) 22–23, 64

Xi Jinping 1, 51, 101

Yang Honggang 31

Zhang Kunmin 24, 27

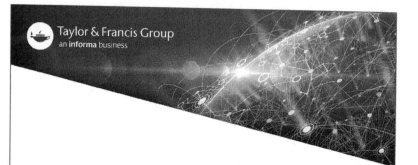